To Teresa for showing me I had wings

and

Nina for pushing me out of the nest

DON'T EVEN THINK OF RAINING ON MY PARADE

Adventures of
The SECRET SOCIETY
OF HAPPY PEOPLE

PAM JOHNSON
FOUNDER

PJ Press, Dallas

Don't Even Think of Raining on My Parade
Adventures of the Secret Society of Happy People

Copyright © 2000 by Pam Johnson
All rights reserved

See Permissions page for permission to use other writers' copyrighted
material in this book.

ISBN 0-9678066-7-4

Library of Congress Card Number: 99-091937

PJ Press   5330 N. MacArthur Blvd. Suite 148-215
                      Irving, Texas   75038   USA

                      972-471-1485   800-291-3068

First Edition: 2000

Johnson, Pam
Don't Even Think of Raining on my Parade:
Adventures of the Secret Society of Happy People / by Pam Johnson

p.cm.
Includes bibliographical references and sources
ISBN 0-9678066-7-4

Book cover design by David C. Perry

DON'T EVEN THINK OF RAINING ON MY PARADE

Adventures of The SECRET SOCIETY OF HAPPY PEOPLE

CONTENTS

Acknowledgements   ix

Introduction   1

Part One   5
The Adventures of
the Secret Society of Happy People

Part Two   103
How Many Types of Happiness Are There?
Let Me Count the Smiles

Epilogue   181

About Us   186

About the Author   189

Permissions   190

Acknowledgements

When you look back to the beginning of an adventure like the Secret Society of Happy People, you realize that it's the result of the collective efforts of so many people. And without the Secret Society of Happy People, this book wouldn't have been written. So, I'd like to thank the following people:

Teresa Dominy and Nina Diamond for being my friends, mentors, and cheerleaders.

The initial brainstormers, creators, and maintainers of the Society: David Perry, Amy Fisher, Rose Yates, Andre Friedmann, Brian Hammer, Gary Schwartz, and Nick Ghanbari.

Of course, so many friends have done more than one thing to support me and the adventures of the Society and this book: stuffing envelopes, listening to me, proofreading, and a million other things, but most important encouraging me to follow my dream. My heartfelt gratitude goes to: Kim Glasgow, Annie Garza, Beth Varma, Melissa Hammer, Debby Nadeau, Mini Dority, Mike and Mary Voigt, Cindy Fitzhugh, Rusty Williamson, Christine DeLorey, Serena and Tom Hawley, Joan Teeter, and Jay Weathermon.

Those who have contributed their personal stories include Hannah Adkins, London Dority, Richard Greene, Lorraine Jackson, Chris Cummings, Terrill Fisher, and Jamie Burleson.

Then there are my friends who've helped shape, mold, and support me through my journey called life. Many of my happy experiences are a result of my friendships with Tonna Rutherford Amos, Robin Read Harrison, Karen Jowers Tarter, Larry Hajovsky, Cindy Vera, Chris Tropeck, Jan and David Lerner, Lynne Hale, Mark Fontaine, Joe Piazza, Ron Pope, Randi Press, Srikant Varma, Rizwain Uquaili, Darren Waxman, and Bill Hill.

Special appreciation to Shirley Keeting, Jim Young, Lisa Walker, and Ron Standifer for believing in the mission of the Society.

This book wouldn't have been created without the wisdom of Erica Rauzin, Kristal Leebrick, Regula Noetzli, and Jamie Guttrich.

Ironically it's also important to thank Ann Landers and all of the governors who responded to our request for a proclamation for National Admit You're Happy Day. They were the unknowing (and perhaps unwilling) catalysts for generating publicity about the Society and our mission. There are too many journalists who reported stories about the Society to thank all of them individually, but I'd like to thank Liz Stevens, Robert G. Wieland, Michael Precker, David Flick, Megan K. Stack, Don Oldenburg, and Ellise Pierce for writing stories that so many people read and embraced.

Of course, special thanks to Bill Maher, Scott Carter, and Dawn DeFalco from *Politically Incorrect* for seeing the merit of the Society's message.

Then there are those people from my younger years who gave me the courage and inspiration to find my dream and follow it: Teannie McCarty, Dorothy Hester, Larry Gill, Bob Blanchette, and the late Louise Green.

And finally thanks to my family, who's life long influence has allowed me to become who I am: my mother, Mary Lafferty Denhart; my dad, Jerry Johnson, and his wife, Kay; my brother, Michael Johnson; my aunts, Linda Moore and Barbara Bates; and my late grandparents, L.D. and Ione Lafferty, Marcus and Jewel Johnson, and Mary Lou Johnson.

Last, thanks to the thousands of people who've contacted the Society, shared their thoughts and stories, and believe in our message.

Introduction

*Now and then it's good to pause in our pursuit of happiness
and just be happy.*

Anonymous

Introduction

The message of the Secret Society of Happy People is simple: When you're happy and you know it, talk about it. Our membership slogan is: Are you happier than you admit you are?

The keyword is *admit*. If you're happy with sixty, seventy, or eighty percent of your life, then shouldn't it get at least fifty percent of your conversation time? Are you one of those people who talks about happiness but has been met with the parade-raining syndrome? You know, the backlash you get from those people who don't want to hear your happy news.

Either way, have you stopped talking about your happy moments?

My only goal when I started the Secret Society of Happy People was to encourage people to talk more about happiness when they were happy and to remind them not to rain on other people's parades. I pictured the Society as a *Dilbert* of happiness. Something funny and amusing but with an inspirational message.

The Society just wanted to make the conversation of happiness chic again; however, in my wildest dreams I never imagined the adventures the Society would experience as it evolved, grew, and became a consumer advocate for the right to express happiness without a social backlash from people who don't want to hear your happy news.

In our first year, we publicly challenged Ann Landers "when she told people to keep their happy news to themselves and not to include happy newsletters with holiday cards," in her November 29, 1998 column. The Society announced the Top Ten Happiest Events and Moments of 1998 and 1999. We created dilemmas for many governors when we declared August 8, 1998, "National Admit You're Happy Day" and asked for official proclamations (which most governors would not issue, and for some awfully bizarre reasons, as you'll see). The Society organized national voting for the Top Ten Happiest Events, Inventions, and Social Changes of the Century from a list of 100 choices, which *Parade* magazine named the "Best List of the Century" on Sunday, December 26, 1999.

When I appeared on ABC's *Politically Incorrect with Bill Maher*, I learned just how controversial expressing happiness can be, and just how misunderstood. You'll read about that here too.

Every time the Society made the news (whether print or broadcast), we were contacted by thousands of people who embraced our message and applauded our efforts. They understand what it feels like to tell someone about something happy and then have their parades rained on. But we also received some not-so-happy messages from "parade-rainers." We'll share a range of responses with you.

The Society isn't here to make you be happy, or to suggest you pretend that you're happy if you're not. Life will always be full of frustrations and problems. While we can't always control our experiences, we can control our responses, reactions, and our sense of perspective. If there is only one single, small happy moment in your day, cherish it. Nurture it. Maybe it will grow.

Sometimes the experience of happiness can just be about recognizing it. In Part II, we introduce twenty-one Types of Happiness. I know, you've never thought of happiness that way.

Don't Even Think of Raining on My Parade is about the birth and true adventures of the Secret Society of Happy People. The more you read, the more you'll see how some people, unfortunately, think *happy* is a four-letter word. You'll also have an opportunity to expand your view of how broad the experience of happiness can be.

Part One

The Adventures of
the Secret Society of Happy People

We all live with the objective of being happy;
our lives are all different and yet the same.

Anne Frank

April 1997

*Happiness is not the absence of conflict,
but the ability to cope with it.*

Anonymous

For the past few years I've been teaching personal empowerment workshops, and I had a couple of articles published.
It's my catalyst for trying to understand how personal power and
destiny co-exist. It's hard to reconcile the two opposite philosophies
that dominate personal growth: "Go with the flow" and "Take charge
of your life." How do we make them work together?

The foundation of the workshops and writing is my version of the
Seven Steps to Personal Empowerment:

Step One
Take Responsibility for Your Life

Accept that you and you alone are responsible for your life.
You have the power to stay where you are or make changes.
You are the one who will have to live
with the consequences of your decisions.

Step Two
Define Your Values and Goals

What is most important to you?
You must define your values and set your goals accordingly.

Step Three
Work through Your Fear

If parts of your life aren't working, then you are probably angry, frustrated, or feeling helpless—either consciously or subconsciously. The underlying cause for most negative feelings is "fear"— fear you will or will not succeed, fear of abandonment, and fear of not being loved. You may need counseling or a support group to process your emotions, but don't ignore them. Suppressed emotions always show up in our lives. They prevent us from making positive changes and forming empowering relationships.

Step Four
Prioritize Your Goals

Decide what goal or goals are the most important to you. Prioritize and take steps to achieve your most important goals.

Step Five
Set Appropriate Boundaries

Once you know what goals you want to accomplish, set boundaries that allow you to do that. It may mean spending less time on the phone talking to friends about what does or doesn't work in your life, managing your time better in the office, or making a date with yourself. Recognize that the choices you make will enable you to achieve the goals you want most.

Step Six
Create a Balanced Life

Take time for your significant other, family, friends, career, and volunteer work, but don't forget you. By keeping your life balanced, not putting too much emphasis on one aspect, it is easier to accept changes because you have a support system in place.

Step Seven
Apply Steps One through Six Daily

Life is continually changing and each day you have to meet the
challenges and opportunities. Your values and goals will change
depending on what's going on around you. So be flexible and
re-evaluate what's important to you. Empowerment is a journey of
evolution that can change from day to day or even moment to
moment. Give yourself permission to enjoy it.

∗

Several people who had attended the workshops suggested that I
start publishing a personal empowerment newsletter. Since so many
newsletters are already on the market, I hesitated. But one weekend,
just for fun, I thought about what I'd put in a newsletter. I know that
true personal empowerment is about transcending emotional wounds
and obstacles; not forgetting them, but allowing them to heal or learning to peacefully co-exist with them. Since humor is essential to healing, the only thing I knew I wanted to include in the newsletter was a
humor column.

I mentally began composing my hypothetical editor's column by
quoting author Caroline Myss. Her coined word, *woundology*, typifies
the intimacy language of the 1990s, which has taken over our conversations. I wondered, in this era of woundology, where were all the
happy people? After all, wasn't the purpose of empowerment to
enable you to experience happiness?

∗

Most Americans live blessed lives. That doesn't mean we have
painless lives, but we do have opportunities and resources many people encounter only in their dreams. So I wondered, where were the
people who liked to talk about their happiness and who wanted to listen to others talk about their happiness?

Then, in my imagination, I saw them: They were standing in a
room telling each other about their happy moments. They happily listened to others. They weren't judging or analyzing the conversations.

11

They were just enjoying the moment. They didn't use their names. They were even wearing Mardi Gras masks, so their identities would stay secret, just in case a parade-rainer (someone who doesn't like happy news) crashed the gathering. Then I saw their banner—they were members of the Secret Society of Happy People.

This daydream made me laugh. I wondered if these meetings existed anywhere except in my imagination. Then it dawned on me. This would be the first humor piece in a newsletter: a profile of the Secret Society of Happy People—people who encourage expressing happiness and discourage "parade-raining."

I'm keenly aware of the parade-raining syndrome that has taken America by storm. In the most recent workshop I taught, when we got to the goal-setting section, an attractive, forty-ish woman named Jan said, "I hate this part." I didn't know why, because I knew she had goals. She wanted to travel abroad and take a class. She had a spirit of adventure. So, I asked her, "Why do you hate this part?"

Jan quickly responded, "Because I don't have any *good* goals. I love my husband and we've been married 18 years. My kids are good—I mean they're kids and they aren't always perfect, but they're good. I'm at a point in my career where I'm content and I'm not trying to climb the ladder of success, so my goals aren't any good."

All I could think was, "If I only had your life." I felt sad that we live in a world where people are made to feel that their goals aren't "good enough." Who decides what goals someone should have? Shouldn't the essence of any goal be to achieve happiness? Anyway, the group discussed Jan's concerns about "good goals," and she became excited as it became clear that her goals were good for her because they made her happy. However, the incident kept replaying in my mind.

This "parade-raining" syndrome has hit me personally too. I'm innately upbeat; I'm often called a Pollyanna. People ask me, "Were you a high school cheerleader?" (Nope) "Are you always full of this much energy?" (Yep) The questions aren't a problem; it's the tone of voice of the inquisitors. It's rarely complimentary.

Of course, I can complain and whine with the best of them. But once I've said my peace I try to find solutions and move forward. It doesn't always happen. Like everyone else, I can fall into the complaining and whining trap and forget to focus on the things that make me happy.

I remember when I got out of college, my roommate, Mary, and I decided to quit gossiping. It was hard, but we did it. Of course, sometimes we'd go out with our friends, come home and find ourselves totally unable to think of anything to say! Why did we do it?

Because, even then, I realized that gossiping was wasted conversation. Now, I'm asking, when—and why—did the majority of our conversations start focusing on what's wrong and ignoring what's right?

During the last 20 years, Americans have gone from keeping our wounds and problems a secret to keeping our happiness a secret. Neither extreme is healthy or useful, but now it's more chic to talk about annoyances, mishaps, and traumas instead of happiness.

People shouldn't ignore or minimize their problems; that's unhealthy and prevents you from working your way back around to happiness. But as it became politically correct to talk about our wounds, it became politically incorrect to talk about being happy.

May 1997

It is not easy to find happiness in ourselves,
and it is not possible to find it elsewhere.

Agnes Repplier

The thought of a group, real or imagined, called the Secret Society of Happy People makes me ponder the whole happiness experience. What is happiness? Where do we find it? Is happiness a constant state of being? Is it really about your personal choice? Can you just say, "Hey, I'm going to be happy," and then be done with it, or is it harder than that? What makes me happy? Is it the same things that make other people happy? And, looking around at the culture we live in, when did we start judging everyone else's happiness?

I think about how babies are usually in a state of happiness unless they're hungry, wet, tired, or hurt. Of course, once the unhappy experience is over, they almost immediately bounce back to their original joyous selves. Even small children can be unhappy one moment and happy in the next. By the time they reach school age they begin judging happiness in a different way. It's judged based on exterior things that people perceive will create a happy feeling. Since happiness comes from within, the exterior things that we believe will make us happy are fleeting moments.

Babies and small children seem to naturally recognize this. Whether they're in a happy or unhappy moment anyone around them knows it. They don't cling to any of the moments longer than they actually last. It's a go-with-the-flow attitude. So if it's our natural instinct to live in the moment as babies and small children, when does this get lost?

Happiness at any age is just a moment. It's not a constant feeling or experience.

It might be several moments linked together, but in the end it is only a series of moments. Some moments my happiness is defined by achieving a goal. Other moments it is defined by seeing something sweet. On occasion, it is even about just doing nothing. And, also, my idea of happiness can change from moment to moment.

The real question is, "Do I recognize happy moments as easily as I recognize unhappy or annoying ones?" Why does a rude driver on the freeway get more of my attention than a friendly cashier at the grocery store? After all, each moment takes the same amount of time and has the same significance in my day.

I'm also recognizing that when people talk about happy things, others don't usually chime in with their happy experiences. But, if someone complains, they create a feeding frenzy of commiseration.

Imagine walking into your office and complaining about your marriage. People just can't talk enough. But, if you walk in, beam at everyone in view, and announce that you're the luckiest person in the world to be married to your spouse, you'll probably reduce the room to complete silence, people rolling back their eyes with jealousy, disgust, or disinterest. Others may walk away or zing you: "Yeah, right. We don't want to know how good you have it." or "I don't want to hear it."

People just can't rain on your parade fast enough. For some time now, our culture has allowed the parade-rainers to define socially acceptable conversation. Mostly, it's whine, complain, and attack. It's common for happy people (or people who are simply blessed with pleasant dispositions, no matter what their life story) to hear, "Are you always this perky?" and "Could you tone it down a bit?" But how often do we say to a parade-rainer, "Are you always this cranky?" or "Could you try to be just a little more upbeat?"

Of course, no one is happy all the time; but when you are happy, it should be okay to talk about it with the same zest and enthusiasm you would your "wounds," and for others to embrace your happiness or at the very least be neutral and say nothing.

In a world where there are more than one hundred Twelve Step groups that give people permission to have and heal wounds, and where there are more how-to-find-happiness books, programs, and seminars than a person can count. I wonder, "Why there isn't a group that stands for just being happy for the sake of happiness?"

Since it's not chic to talk about happiness, people feel guilty when they experience it. They may even rain on their own parades, so other people won't do it for them. When we lose the ability to be happy for ourselves, it's impossible to be truly happy for others. How can we give something away that we don't have?

Has it always been this way? Or have we just forgotten how to talk about happiness? What societal forces have encouraged the general acceptance of chronic crankiness? It can't be just one thing. It's far more complex. We live in a culture where self-help is prominent in publishing, on daytime TV, and talk radio. Our conversations center around analyzing everything. The advertising that surrounds us creates false needs and wishes. We are bombarded twenty-four hours a day with bad news. Politicians campaign on the "what's wrong" platform. No wonder we barely recognize our happy moments.

✳

Although the self-help movement began in the 1930s, it was private. People were encouraged to keep their identities anonymous because it wasn't socially acceptable to have problems.

This wasn't healthy for anyone, but now the pendulum seems to have swung the other way. By the 1980s, it became not only socially acceptable but in some cases even chic to participate in self-help programs. But at last, it was okay to admit that we had problems and were trying to solve or recover from them.

TV and radio talk shows started bringing self-help right into our living rooms, offices, and cars. The electronic talk sessions have become free therapy for millions. In fact, if you can't think of an emotional wound you might have—or if you think you've moved on just fine, thank you—just watch enough TV and listen to the radio and you'll come up with a dandy worry soon enough. Bookstores are lined with books that tell you what's wrong with your life and how you can repair it by following their simple programs. And, of course, any given day, the so-called experts hold more seminars and lectures than anyone can count, about how to fix your life (broken, just a little chipped, cracked, or not).

On the other hand, once we become aware of an emotional wound, we do need to talk about it and we should. That is how we can find solutions or allow wounds to heal. People shouldn't have to hide their human flaws and tragedies. Everyone has suffered through some.

But "it's okay" seems to have become "it's mandatory." Somewhere along the way we began to focus only on the wounds. That was an unhealthy turn in the road. The purpose of acknowledging and treating your wounds is to allow them to heal. Then, you can transcend or peacefully co-exist with the pain they've caused you, so that happiness can be part of your life.

✳

Self-help alone isn't responsible for making complaining chic. Consumerism also plays a hefty role. Advertising constantly reminds us that we'd be happier if we would only buy this or that. It's everywhere: TV, radio, magazines, web pages, billboards, newspapers, events, airports, taxis, buses, and even at the movie theatres.

If you're honest, you'll recognize that you buy many products and services because you think they will give you a moment of happiness, maybe more. The ads promise us acceptance, beauty, love, social status, professional success and better hair days.

Nothing is wrong with buying things and enjoying them; just recognize why you're buying them. Even when you purchase one of these happy carrots, you rarely allow yourself to enjoy it before you're off chasing the next happy carrot. Most of the time the carrots only represent illusions of happiness.

We focus on what we're trying to acquire, instead of recognizing and smiling about what we already have.

The concept that we "need to buy" this or that to find happiness keeps us chasing it. Have we been brainwashed by the advertising industry? Commercials are great when they inform the consumer about choices. But has the objective of giving consumers knowledge about choices been completely replaced by creating perceived "needs?"

✳

And last, but not least—you can't forget the wonderful world of politics.

When was the last time you heard a political campaign slogan that said, "Life is pretty darn good and our problems are manageable. So if you're happy with the way things are, elect me." NEVER!

Instead, politicians seem to run on platforms that focus on the worst, platforms that are designed to scare you into voting for them and their solutions. It is hard to tell if they have any real interest in solving the problems or if their only goal is to get you to actually go to the polls and vote for them.

Politicians do want your vote, so they focus on what's wrong and their promises to fix it. Even when they run for re-election they still focus on "what's wrong" instead of "what they accomplished." Since most politicians wouldn't run an ad that hadn't been seen by a focus group, I have to wonder if the ads are what they want to say, or what they think we want to hear.

✳

When I tell people about my newest idea for a humor piece, a profile about the Secret Society of Happy People, they laugh and say, "Let me know when you start it, I want to join."

I guess I'm beginning to understand why there's a need for the Secret Society of Happy People. Maybe it's time for someone to invite us to notice our happy times and savor them and talk about them.

July 1997

What is the worth of anything,
But for the happiness it will bring?

Richard Owen Cambridge

Ifeel as if a happy angel is sitting on my shoulder whispering in my ear: the Secret Society of Happy People. The idea won't leave my mind.

I really don't want to start a club, but what do I want? I haven't written the humor piece or started the empowerment newsletter either. I'm not sure why. When I think of the Society I see it as an organization, more than a humor essay.

Happy awareness keeps haunting me. I realize that we understand our constitutional right to "pursue happiness," but we're just not sure what to do once we've caught it. That doesn't make any sense, because isn't finding happiness the reason why we do most of the things we do?

How many people do you know (even the cranky ones) who get up in the morning and say, "I wonder what I can do today to make myself miserable?" Misery isn't exactly a conscious goal, but I suspect if aliens eavesdropped on us they'd think we were a species that specialized in it.

Only recently has road rage, children shooting children in schools, and disgruntled workers "going postal" become a regular part of the daily news. Although every new story comes with words of shock and dismay, in reality we're rarely surprised anymore, unless of course these things happen in our own backyard. Then the reality of these horrors is too large to be shielded by even the best defense

19

mechanisms. We really hope and believe that these senseless tragedies will only happen somewhere else. Or not at all—at least not again.

History is full of horrendous murders, social injustices, and robberies by pirates, bandits, and gangs. In all likelihood, these events will be part of the human experience for the foreseeable future. Until recently these behaviors have been limited to a select few antisocial personalities. Most people, even when angry, do not act violently. But now, if you cross someone, you don't know if you'll be looking down the barrel of a gun. During the past twenty years, the expression of hostility has taken on a new face. It no longer belongs solely to one of those statistically rare, antisocial "crazies." Today, the seemingly average guy on the street is apparently just as likely to injure or kill.

On a less violent, but just as common, note, we've also forgotten that our actions always have an impact on others. Maybe *It's a Wonderful Life* should be required viewing for school children: It shows that even when we don't think our actions, our words, and deeds impact others, they really do.

What happened to the old adage, "If you can't say something nice about someone don't say anything at all?" When did it become, "If you can't complain or whine, then don't say anything at all?"

Maybe it should just be, "If you can't say anything nice, then just don't rain on someone else's parade."

August 1997

*The really happy person
is the one who can enjoy the scenery
while on a detour.*

Anonymous

In my new state of "happy awareness," from both a personal and cultural perspective, I understand that we don't live in a perfect world. We still have challenges ahead of us before mankind can enter utopia. I know people have problems and aren't happy twenty-four hours a day—that's not possible or realistic. But I'm also becoming even more aware of how we don't talk about our happy moments in lieu of whining and complaining. It's not that happy moments don't exist, but they're not valued as highly as unhappy ones.

I suspect that, at least in America, most of us have more happy moments than unhappy ones. Shouldn't happiness get at least half of our conversation time? Am I the only one who recognizes this? What am I supposed to do about it? Is this that famous line "a little knowledge can be a dangerous thing"?

Sometimes I want this new awareness to go away. Ignorance is bliss, but once it's lost you can't get it back. So, what does moving forward mean? Am I really going to start the Secret Society of Happy People?

21

November 1997

*The great essentials to happiness in this life are
something to do, something to love, and something to hope for.*

Joseph Addison

I'm sitting in my living room when Kim, my neighbor, drops by and announces that she's going to audition the next night as the lead singer in a rock and roll band.

Kim won't even sing karaoke at a friend's party, so my first thought is, "I didn't even know you liked to sing." My next thought is, "Do you know how hard it is to be in a rock and roll band?"

I catch myself in midthought before I say a word. I realize she isn't asking for my opinion. She's sharing her dream. Any negative comment I make, even if it comes from concern for her well-being, would be raining on her parade.

Aren't our biggest regrets not pursuing our dreams?

I happily agree to go with her to the audition.

It's so easy to rain on someone's parade even if you don't intend to.

January 1998

Plenty of people miss their share of happiness,
not because they never found it,
but because they didn't stop to enjoy it.

W. Feather

I've spent the past few months trying to forget the Secret Society of Happy People. It's a funny concept. A group of people talking about their happy events and moments. The Society won't tell you what makes you happy or how to find happiness. They will just appreciate it and talk about it when it shows up.

Could this organization get people to recognize that happiness is a moment, just like unhappiness? Happiness is something to value. It is precious, moment by moment.

But to start a club like that. It'd be so much work! I have a more than full-time job—when would I have the time? What would the club do? Who has time for meetings? How about a club without meetings? That could make some people very happy.

February 1998

*I don't know what your destiny will be, but one thing I do know:
The only ones among you who will be really happy
are those who have sought and found how to serve.*

Albert Schweitzer

I surrender. I'm now dreaming about the Secret Society of Happy People. It's been almost a year since I first thought of it and now it doesn't leave my thoughts.

Capitulation is my only alternative. I guess the first thing I need to do is get a logo designed.

Meanwhile, of course, my brother, Michael, ribs me that he's decided to start the Society of Publicly Pissed-Off People. He thinks he'll have more members than I will.

I wanted to respond, "You don't need a club because your members already have a voice that's heard all of the time."

But even he concedes that you can't say the Secret Society of Happy People without grinning.

March 1998

Happiness:
it lies in the joy of achievement,
in the thrill of the creative effort.

Franklin Delano Roosevelt

Now that I've made the decision to officially start the Secret Society of Happy People, what's next? I'm not sure what we'll do, but we'll be the antidote for the complaining, whining, and the woundology movement.

Mission:	Be the voice for the expression of happiness.
Slogan:	Are You Happier Than You Admit You Are?
Membership Goodies:	T-shirt, lapel pin (so we can recognize each other), bumper sticker, quarterly newsletter.
Meetings:	Optional. If members (or nonmembers) want to start meetings they can, but it's not a requirement because meetings can make some people unhappy.

My friend, Kim, suggests that each member should get another member as a pen pal so they can connect with other happy people. I like the idea. Members will have the option to have a pen or e-mail pal.

Still, it is a secret society, so maybe some people will want to keep their identities a "secret." Maybe we should have decoder rings or even a secret handshake?

June 1998

The foolish man seeks happiness in the distance;
The wise grows it under his feet.

James Openheim

I finally got my logo. I love it! It brings a smile to my face. The logo shows three smiling faces, done in black and pink. I'm not sure men will like the pink, but I'm also not sure that they're my target audience.

I'm beginning to order the membership items. My Dad and his wife, Kay, gave me a small loan, so I could buy enough T-shirts, lapel pins, and bumper stickers to get discounts.

Now I just have to find a place to store the stuff until I start getting members.

My friends and colleagues are also supporting this idea. Lots of my friends are donating their time to design and maintain the web site, editing everything, graphic design, data base administration, stuffing and mailing envelops. Apparently I know lots of secretly or not-so-secretly happy people.

July 1998

Happiness sneaks through a door you didn't know you left open.

John Barrymore

I just received my first promotional mailing piece from the printer. Now the Society is official, or at least it feels that way.

Will people think it's funny? Or fun? Will they get the message? Will they join? What will happen next?

I'm starting to get real excited. I'm glad I did this. I wish I would have done it sooner.

My first official mailing—an explanation about the Society and an invitation to join—was sent thanks to the help of my friends, Annie and Beth.

The web site just went up too. It explains our philosophy, how to become a member, and has a place for people to post their happy news and thoughts.

August 1998

Happiness is like a kiss. You must share it to enjoy it.

Bernard Meltzner

Ijust returned from a business trip, and there it was in the mail: our first official member!!! She's someone from Kansas, somebody I don't even know!

This is so exciting because a total stranger likes the concept of the Society. It's confirmed. They're out there: a group of not-so-secretly happy people.

October 1998

Happiness is like jam...
You can't spread even a little without getting some on yourself.

Vern McLellan

About 25 people from all over the country have joined the Secret Society of Happy People. It's exciting. I'm writing the Society's first newsletter. I'm also going to send out our first press release...maybe a reporter will think our group is funny and do a story.

November 1998

It is the inalienable right of all to be happy.

Elizabeth Cady Stanton

We're getting a few members each week. I think we have around forty.

I went to my dad's for Thanksgiving. When I was there I got a message from a reporter from the *Fort Worth Star-Telegram*. I immediately called her back and she wants to do a story about the Society. I'm so excited. Our first story. I sent her an e-mail with more details about the Society and she also wants to talk to a couple of Society members.

When the reporter interviews me, she keeps trying to get me to say that the Society tells people to "be happy," but we don't. I explain that it's about talking more about happiness if you happen to be happy. After a long interview, I think she gets our message. I hope so.

When I get back home on Sunday, I receive calls from a couple of Society members telling me to read today's Ann Landers column (November 29). Someone had written to her complaining about receiving happy holiday newsletters and she responded by telling people not to send them out.

Although parade-raining is prevalent in our culture, even pervasive, it still shocked me to see such a public display of it, especially from a respected advice columnist, such as Ann Landers, of all people. Why didn't Ann just tell people that if they don't want to read happy holiday newsletters, they can just throw them away? After all, there's no troop of holiday newsletter police waiting to give you a ticket if you don't read them.

The Society members felt that we should respond and ask her to apologize to all the holiday letter writers she made feel bad for wanting to share happy news. She's raining on their parades.

I decided that responding is an appropriate thing for the Society to do, but how? Is it such a great idea to take on the opinion of Ann Landers, such a public figure, so well-liked, for this major dose of holiday parade-raining?

If we're going to speak up we have to do it quick. But the last thing the Society needs is a public enemy with a daily column millions of people read. Of course, our response might be met with complete silence, because no one is interested.

December 1998

This time, like all times, is a very good one,
if we but know what to do with it.

Ralph Waldo Emerson

I sent a response overnight to Ann Landers and her syndicate service. I also canceled a business trip, began writing my press release, and put together a press kit to be faxed.

At that moment I quit being logical and started following my gut instincts. I call more than 100 newspapers to get fax numbers and the names of editors. I was up all night faxing my press kit to them.

When I called the newspapers the next day, I found that most of the people who I spoke to didn't get the release or, at least, hadn't seen it. So I spent the day doing follow-up phone calls, trying to convince reporters that this story is worth covering and worked into the night refaxing everyone. This story has humor, fame, personality, controversy, and Christmas cheer, and so clearly illustrates the Society's message. What more could the press want?

Of course I sent a copy of our press release to the reporter from the *Fort Worth Star-Telegram* who had already interviewed me about the Society. She says she'll add it to her story, which is scheduled to run on Thursday.

I'm so busy that in some ways the week feels like it's flying by. On the other hand, it seems like Thursday will never get here. Waiting for a story to appear is so nerve-wracking. Too bad they don't let you read it before it runs.

After what feels like hundreds of phone calls, I find a reporter at the Dallas office of the Associated Press who thinks our Ann Landers rebuttal is funny. He tries contacting Ann Landers, but her office won't call him back. Then he's off work for a couple of days, so my story is just sitting there.

I continued to spend my days on the phone and evenings faxing. I'm grateful that I can take vacation time from my "day job" as a sales rep for a publishing company.

I'm exhausted beyond belief and very unsure whether our message will get out, but only time will tell.

A reporter from the *Dallas Morning News* calls about the Ann Landers story. He wants to come to my house to interview me about it. Is my work starting to pay off?

With all this midnight faxing and daytime phoning, I haven't had time to decorate my home for the holidays. It looks so bare, not a bit like the home of a person who encourages people to express happiness. I called my friends and they assembled for an emergency holiday decorating evening. By midnight, the tree was decorated with its usual purple, white, and silver ornaments, bows and white lights, an *It's A Wonderful Life* village lines the bar, and a snowman collection completes the "winter wonderland" theme.

The *Fort Worth Star-Telegram* story runs. Immediately, the flood of e-mails and phone calls start. I drop off a copy of the story for the AP reporter and start faxing it to the other newspapers I've been courting. I'm incoherent from sleep deprivation. But, finally, the Society is getting some results. Newspaper coverage lends credibility to our message.

Then I get brave and reach beyond the newspapers. I fax the press release and a copy of the *Star-Telegram* story to the national late night television shows. I thought this story would be perfect to include in an opening monologue.

Nevertheless, there's no one more surprised than me when I get a call from an assistant at *Politically Incorrect with Bill Maher*. She wants to know if I have a videotape. I don't. Of course, I couldn't tell her that, so I just promise to get one to her ASAP. I immediately get back on the phone and pitch the story to the local newscasts.

Thank goodness there wasn't a major news story going on. Two stations schedule interviews for that weekend.

The *Star-Telegram* story starts running in other newspapers around the country.

The AP reporter is back at work and plans to write our story immediately, so I take an update to him. While I'm at the AP office, he has the photographer take my picture. He tells me this story will be sent to the New York Associated Press office Saturday morning. If they pick it up, it will hit the wire Saturday afternoon, in time for Sunday newspapers.

Saturday afternoon I went shopping for something new to wear for my first TV interview, and I got a message from the BBC in London requesting a radio interview. This is my first clue that we've hit the international Associated Press broadcast wire.

At last, the ball is really rolling.

Sunday morning, the AP story is printed in thousands of papers across the country. Literally hundreds of e-mails arrive.

As the week unfolds, more than 40,000 people contact the Society through our web site. Several people send e-mails and letters saying that they are grateful to see our story because they were halfway through writing their holiday newsletters, and quit because of Ann Landers' column. After they read about the Society, they decide to send their newsletters as usual. This surprises me. How could one person (even advice "institution" Ann Landers) have so much influence over people, that they'd actually not send their happy holiday newsletters when they really wanted to?

Even a reporter tells me he was considering taking a pass on writing his holiday newsletter because of the Ann Landers' column, however, he still believed his readers understood that Ann was saying "don't brag," not don't write.

I couldn't believe what I was hearing.

I hadn't really thought of the Society in serious political terms. My serious thoughts had been on the psychological and sociological side, mostly a sense that we all need to rebel against the over-expression of woundology. But, at this point, it becomes clear that the Society is also about the right to free speech, the right to communicate about happiness.

The number of web site visitors continues to climb by the thousands. Hundreds of people join the Society.

Hundreds more write us and send faxes. Most of the messages are supportive, but we get our fair share of unhappy messages. A common one is, "How dare you charge $30 for happiness?" I only wish that for $30 I could give someone happiness—I'd be able to take over the Prozac market!

It's ironic because if I were selling a "way to happiness" or something to enhance complaining and whining, no one would question paying for whatever I was selling.

In response, I prepare a standard answer politely explaining that the $30 is for the membership stuff—a T-shirt, lapel pin, bumper sticker, newsletter, and an e-mail or pen pal. But anyone can participate in the message of the Society without the membership stuff. I invite them to join our e-mail circle because it's free.

I'm disappointed and frustrated that people are so mean, when all I'm trying to do is get them to talk more about being happy, if they happen to be happy. If they want the stuff, great, but they don't need it to appreciate the message. They just need to recognize a moment of happiness and have the urge to share it.

Some messages are from people who just hate the whole idea of the Society. One says, "In the future, people would take further retaliatory actions than sending an e-mail." I found this very disturbing.

Resourceful producers find my phone number and start calling to schedule radio interviews. I did somewhere between twenty and thirty radio interviews around the world. We're getting a lot of responses from everyone except Ann Landers. I wonder if she will apologize to the happy holiday newsletter writers. I check her column daily looking for a response. I don't see one.

I'm anxiously waiting for the *Dallas Morning News* story to run. What will they write?

Mid-December becomes a blur. I respond to people who are interested in the Society, try not to be upset by people who don't like us, and field calls from reporters. I can't remember the last time I was so tired or exhilarated. Thousands of people embrace and applaud our message. For everyone who contacts us, I wonder, how many more have started applying the philosophy of the Society in their conversations? Maybe millions.

The following Monday, December 14, the *Dallas Morning News* runs its story. It focuses on the Ann Landers incident. They interviewed her. She told them she wouldn't respond to us by apologizing to people who like to send or read happy holiday newsletters. Well, at least, there was a response, but it wasn't what we wanted. Ann still thought her comments were appropriate! How was that possible?

Apparently, in a 1993 column, Ann told people if they didn't like holiday newsletters to "trash 'em." Why is she telling people who want to share happy news to just keep it to themselves? Isn't telling happy news a pretty harmless activity in the grand scheme of life? Shouldn't people who are happy be encouraged to spread the joy around? Are people so jealous and resentful that all happy news seems like "bragging"?

The *Dallas Morning News* story also includes my home office telephone number. People who hate happy holiday newsletters call me. When I calmly suggest that they simply throw them away, they become furious, yelling profanities before hanging up. When I'm away or on the other line, they leave hostile messages saying, "Don't you know some people didn't have a happy year?" and "How dare you tell people to write those newsletters?"

Fortunately, I also receive several e-mails, letters, and phone calls from people who like reading and writing holiday newsletters.

The happy message board on the web site gets lots of new postings. Unfortunately many are unhappy, but fortunately there are still more happy ones. However, the unhappy ones really stand out. I'm not sure what to do about this. If I take them down, am I censoring? Don't unhappy people also have the right to free speech? Sure. But it isn't fair to the people who visit the Society's web site because they want to share their happy news but instead find out that the Chronically Cranky got there first.

Maybe I shouldn't be surprised at the negative responses. I don't expect everyone to embrace the message that happiness should be shared, but I am surprised at this kind of hostility. The Society is about trying to create balance between happy and unhappy moments. The Society recognizes that pain, annoyance, and struggle are part of everybody's life, but so is happiness. Why should anyone have to defend the right to express it?

During December, the three stories run throughout the world, including India, Israel, Germany, and Australia. We continue to receive more e-mails and letters.

Many people ask, "Do you have to have a computer to participate?" Of course you don't, just if you want access to the web site. The printed newsletter will keep members updated about the latest

Society news and happenings.

One lady writes, "I had my grandson look up your address on the computer. I'm eighty-six and want to join because I love pen pals."

We receive several calls from men, more than I ever expected. Many men are giving their wives memberships as gifts, but several join themselves. One gentleman tells me, "My wife and I are happily married. We have a hard time finding other couples to talk with about this."

Someone writes a note on a membership application to tell us that her boss had reprimanded her for being "too happy." I hope this is an isolated incident. Is it possible to be "too happy" at work? Wouldn't someone who is happy to be in the office constitute a boss's dream employee? I think people who can be happy at work are living a blessed life. This reminds me of a promotional clip from *Patch Adams*.

It's apparent people crave and appreciate happy news. The Society can be the voice to encourage the expression of happiness. It's clear that there is a role for us, and it's just starting to take shape.

Overall, I am exhilarated to learn that so many people get the Society's message. It makes it worth the sleepless nights and chaotic days. All my doubts about forming the Society are starting to disappear as complete strangers from around the world embrace the message and even say "thank you" for the Society.

I've worked in marketing and public relations, but this time I am dealing with the media about something I've created. It's so different. It's personal, so you want everything to be perfect.

I'm asked the same questions over and over, and I correct the same misunderstandings over and over. I know that part of starting any new organization is explaining its message. I just never realized how difficult that really is. The most commonly asked questions are:

Q – "Why is it a secret?"

A – "It's funny. We're just making a play on words. Because we spend so much time whining and complaining, we've put happiness in the closet. It's become a secret. Happy events and moments have become secrets because we don't talk about them."

Q – "So you want everyone to be happy?"

A – "No, we just want people to talk about it more if they are happy."

Q – "Have you always been a happy person?"

A – "I'm not happy any more or less than anyone else; that's not what this is about. It's about expressing happiness if you are happy, and about discouraging people from raining on other people's parades."

Q – "What do you do to make yourself happy?"

A – "Depends on the moment. Happiness is just a moment, like annoyance. Sometimes I'm happy reading a book, other times I want to be hanging out with my friends, and sometimes I just want an ice cream cone."

Q – "Do you write holiday newsletters?"

A – "That's not really important. What's important is that people have a right to write and send them just like people have a right to read them or throw them away."

Some people have gleaned the faulty impression that I have a charmed life that's problem free. All I can think is "Wake up, Tinkerbell! Nobody has a completely happy life."

I've experienced my share of problems, pain, and annoyances—just like everyone else. My jobs have had their highs and lows; I've eaten spaghetti for a week at a time; family and friends have had illnesses and other problems; I've dealt with car problems and annoying mechanics; I've seen friends come and go; and my heart has been broken.

These experiences aren't representative of my life, however.

That's why I think it's equally important to recognize and talk about the other experiences of my life—including the happy ones.

When I go home to see my dad and Kay (his wife) during the Christmas holidays, I visit one of my old friends. We've known each other since high school. I moved away several years ago, so we only see each other about once a year. These visits are great big catch-up gab sessions. Of course, I share with her how thrilled I am about the number of people who've expressed interest in the Society, become members, and how receptive the media is regarding the Society's message. It's been around the world in less than one month. My friend replies, "When are you going to be in *People*? You're nothing in middle America until you've been in *People*." I'm shocked, hurt, and speechless.

I think, "How ironic that one of my dearest and oldest friends is trying to rain on my parade when I'm out here talking about how people rain on other people's parades!" Her reaction reminds me again that parade-rainers can lurk in anybody's backyard. I wonder if she even realized what she'd done.

I return home and need to amuse myself, so I decide that the Society will announce the Top Ten Happiest Events and Moments of 1998:

10. The Pope visits Cuba. It's the happiest the Cubans have been in forty years.
9. Camryn Manheim wins an Emmy and gleefully accepts "for all the fat girls!"
8. Viagra—need we say more; Propecia—the bald pill; now you've got both ends covered.
7. The McCaughey septuplets celebrate their first birthday.
6. The U.S. Olympic Women's Ice Hockey team wins the first gold medal ever awarded for women's hockey.
5. The VW Beetle returns.
4. Happiest political moment: Jesse "the Gov" Ventura elected in Minnesota.
3. Mark McGwire and Sammy Sosa tie the baseball home run record race. They show happy sportsmanship by being happy for each other. We were happy for them too.
2. At age 77, John Glenn returns to space.

1. The first 14 days in 1998 are very happy because no one has heard of Monica Lewinsky and ignorance is bliss.

The list is fun and proves a point. Remembering happy highlights is a great way to end a year. The list hits the AP broadcast wire and more people contact us.

The Society also presents the "Not Letting Anyone Rain on My Parade" awards. We give them to three people who lived this motto best in 1998: Christopher Reeve, Dr. Patch Adams (the person the movie depicts), and Oprah Winfrey.

We honor Christopher Reeve for continuing to believe he and thousands of others will walk again despite anyone else's pessimism and for his landmark fundraising, research, lobbying, and public education efforts on behalf of spinal cord injuries. His amazing spirit and his insistence upon continuing to live a full personal and professional life inspires everyone.

Dr. Patch Adams is honored for never giving up on his belief that humor and compassion are the cornerstones of healing and for leading the way to humane health care through his Gesundheidt Institute.

We honor Oprah Winfrey for choosing every day to do a show that educates, enlightens, and comforts her viewers despite recent nasty-talk trends and complaints from critics who just don't get what she's doing this season.

I can't believe the enormous response the Society has received from the press and people from around the world. Maybe we really are going to help change the way people express happiness.

January 1999

The secret of happiness is curiosity.

Norman Douglas

To my surprise stories about the Society are published in newspapers around the country, even when they're a month old. I find out when a story runs when I get e-mails and phone calls from people who've read about us.

People from Canada and Australia have joined the Society, so I guess we've become an international organization. We're also getting a lot of e-mails from people in India who want to join, but because of international trade restrictions they can't convert their currency into U.S. dollars—even on credit cards. I'm not sure what to do about this. We just aren't prepared to be international. But we're getting there. I'm quickly learning how to fill out those customs forms for shipping.

People are sending e-mails letting us know about other happy web sites, groups, and organizations. We're getting e-mails from people who are looking for happiness. We don't want to tell people how to find happiness. First of all, we can't. And that isn't our mission: We want people to talk about happiness once they have found it and discourage parade-raining.

Many people will happily tell you how to become happy: family members, friends, self-help experts, TV and radio talk show hosts, newspaper columnists, magazine reporters, clergy, politicians, company spokespeople, and others who are all part of the "don't think for yourself and follow my advice" movement. So, it's clear that "the way to happiness" market is more than saturated.

We're also getting requests for something for kids. I'm sure kids are influenced by the "woundology" and "parade-raining" syndrome. We need to have a nonprofit organization to develop and implement programs for children. It'll be a while before we can afford to put that together—maybe next year.

I just want to slow down enough to find time to reflect on the past month. What does it mean for the Society? I think all of this activity has defined our role as consumer advocates for the personal right to express happiness. Who would have guessed that the expression of happiness would be such a heated topic? Not me.

I balance my day job with the demands of the Society. It's a challenge, but I'm committed to the Society. I believe our message needs to be heard by more people. From the responses we received in December and the messages still being sent, I can tell people are embracing our philosophy and applying it in their lives. Most people who contact us don't actually join. I think they just like knowing that we exist; however, some do want stuff with our logo, they just don't want to be members.

I have received more e-mails and letters from people who have been accused of being "too happy" at work. This really upsets me. Isn't that the ideal work environment: workplaces and jobs that create happiness?

Don't people have the right to express themselves, especially happy expressions, at work without fear of being reprimanded or fired? You'd think that freedom of speech is only controversial if you are saying something negative or inflammatory. But people are getting in trouble for expressing their happiness.

I always thought your right to free speech was protected by the Constitution. Wouldn't that include free speech in the workplace? In your wildest dreams, you'd never think that you'd have to question whether the expression of happiness in the workplace was protected by your constitutional right to free speech.

I call the American Civil Liberties Union (ACLU). I speak with an attorney who specializes in workplace law, "Does it violate a person's civil rights if they are fired for expressing happiness at work?" To my shock, I find out that employers can fire anyone if they don't like something you say. In most cases there isn't any legal protection in the workplace regarding your constitutional right to free speech, including the expression of happiness. The only exception is that some unions have won this protection for their members. So, basically your constitutional right to free speech only protects you from the government. You can't be arrested or fined for something you say, but you can lose your job! I couldn't believe what I'd heard.

In reaction to this revelation I decide to add a section to our web site requesting stories from people who have been discriminated against for expressing happiness. I also want to make people aware that they don't have a constitutional right to free speech at work.

The Society issues a press release asking for stories from people who'd been fired, reprimanded, or discriminated against for express-ing happiness at work. We want to find out the exact extent of this unbelievable problem. We received a little coverage from this release and found out that a lot of people don't like the ACLU or our interest in free speech in the workplace. It's ironic because the ACLU merely works to ensure that the civil rights of U.S. citizens are protected.

But the real heart of this issue is that it's a pathetic social evolu-tion if people in America don't feel they can freely express happiness at work without negative repercussions. We spend a lot of time work-ing. If you happen to like your job, company, or boss; why shouldn't you be able to say so?

How many company presidents would say, "We encourage our employees to be miserable. If you're happy, then you don't fit into our corporate culture." I don't think many executives would consciously promote that philosophy, but that is what's happening—so maybe some do.

When and why has this happened? Has the *Dilbert* principle of absurdity run amuck? Cartoonist Scott Adams makes the absurdities of corporate America tolerable by bringing laughter to the workplace. But have his readers taken the message too much to heart?

Or is it that despite a robust economy, people don't feel they have job security? There was a time when your company and co-workers were like a second family, but now more often than not, your resumé includes many employers, so you don't bond with any particular com-pany or group of co-workers. Some changes are by choice and others are as a result of the downsizing trend.

Or is this just one more reflection of the general promotion of "complaining and whining" that's sweeping the nation? Maybe it's all of the above and more.

*

My hometown newspaper, the *Abilene Reporter News*, just printed a feature story about the Society. It ran in the Sunday edition on the front page of the feature section. The story included a large picture of me. I immediately started receiving calls, e-mails, and letters from people I haven't spoken to in years. They were people I went to school with, former co-workers, and other friends I had lost contact with after I moved away. It was fun, nostalgic, and exciting to reconnect.

However, two of my best friends whom I have kept in touch with on a semiregular basis haven't called or even e-mailed. Maybe they didn't read the story. But wouldn't their parents or some mutual friend mention it to them? It feels like they aren't happy for me.

Nevertheless, I'm not going to let them rain on my parade, because there are so many exciting things happening.

*

A member suggests that we sponsor a National Admit You're Happy Day. Sounds interesting. What would we do and when would it be? Maybe a convention or gathering? We could have a masquerade ball. Too many ideas, not enough time.

I get a note from Patch Adams thanking us for selecting him as one of the recipients of our 1998 awards "For Not Letting Anyone Rain On His Parade." I thought it was really sweet of him to write to us.

A talent coordinator calls from *Politically Incorrect*. She found one of our faxes and thinks our concept is interesting and amusing. I send her a press kit. I'm delighted. If *PI* books me as a guest to represent the Society, then maybe I can get booked on other shows.

I got a call from a member in Kansas, Stephany, who's hosting a Secret Society of Happy People Super Bowl party. She's agreed to be the coordinator for the Kansas City chapter. The Society has its first official chapter.

I'm also interviewed by Nina L. Diamond for her book, *Voices of Truth: Conversations with Scientists, Thinkers and Healers* which will be published by Lotus Press in March 2000. I'm going to be one of fourteen Q & A interviews. We discuss the controversy surrounding happiness and the Society's efforts to create public awareness about the fact an employee's constitutional right to free speech isn't protected in the workplace.

Others in the book are best-selling authors James Redfield, Deepak Chopra, Brian Weiss, physicist Michio Kaku, award-winning former CNN correspondent and novelist Charles Jaco, NASA's JoAnn Morgan, and Arun Gandhi, grandson of Mahatma Gandhi and director of the Gandhi Institute.

February 1999

Don't evaluate your life in terms of achievements....
Instead, wake up and appreciate everything you encounter
along your path.
Enjoy the flowers that are there for your pleasure.
Tune in to the sunrises, the little children,
the laughter, the rain and the birds.
Drink it all in....
There is no way to happiness; happiness is the way.

Dr. Wayne W. Dyer

Happy news! I'm booked to appear on *Politically Incorrect*.
We'll tape the show on March 18, and it airs the next night.
The foil for the Secret Society of Happy People will be comedian
Richard Lewis. His act is based on being depressed and miserable.
They haven't confirmed the other two guests yet. I figure Richard can
whine but he isn't mean, so he's a good choice to represent the view
opposing the Society's message. This should be fun. Besides, since I
saw him on *Anything But Love*, the sitcom with Jamie Lee Curtis, I've
had a little crush on him.

After all, from the Society's perspective, if Richard Lewis is
happy being miserable, then we're happy for him.

Politically Incorrect is one of my favorite shows, and I've always
wanted to be a guest. I've even imagined myself as a guest; I just
never imagined why.

A reporter from *Glamour* calls. They want to mention the
Society in a sidebar in the May issue. The publicity ball just keeps
rolling. I keep doing radio interviews. The December story from the

Fort Worth Star-Telegram keeps running. There is no way to track its path and intercept it, though. If there was, I'd update it. So much has happened in just two months.

I'm obsessing over National Admit You're Happy Day. If we're going to do a convention, we need to book space and start promoting it. Would people actually show up? Where would we have it? Disneyland? Maybe we're not big enough to have a convention just yet. Maybe next year or the one after that.

In an effort to be pro-active about encouraging the expression of happiness in the workplace, I think the Society should develop a program for companies to implement to encourage happy conversations. I believe most companies want their employees to admit it if they are happy.

Unfortunately, some people are expressing that the Society is making them unhappy, because we don't offer a magic solution for finding happiness. Have we moved to a place where people don't want to be responsible for finding their own happiness? Or are they desperately trying to find it?

I think part of the problem is that people don't know how to recognize and identify happiness. So it's impossible for them to seize the moment. They think it's just one feeling. For kicks, I tried to identify ten types of happiness. To my surprise I came up with eighteen (and eventually twenty-one).

Amusement	Exuberance	Peaceful
Anticipation	Fun	Playful
Bittersweet	Giving	Relief
Borrowed	Grateful	Satisfaction
Celebration	Humor	Spiritual
Cheerful	Joyful	Surprise
Contentment	Love	Sweet

This list has been evolving since it began, and I'm sure it will continue to grow.

After I identified the types of happiness, I started thinking about stories I've heard, things that have happened to me, and humor pieces I've read that described each type.

(Part II is all about the twenty-one Types of Happiness).

March 1999

Life is too important to be taken seriously.

Oscar Wilde

I'm totally swamped at my day job. I finally told my boss I'd be taking a couple of vacation days in mid-March. I'm still trying to decide if I should tell him I'm going to be on *Politically Incorrect*.

I'm starting to get really nervous. The talent coordinator tells me that Bill Maher, the host, will play "devil's advocate" and will challenge the Society's views. I believe I can win him over after he understands we're talking about a right to free speech. How do I prepare for a free-for-all show?

When I saw my name in *TV Guide* it hits me; I'm really going to be on *Politically Incorrect*. I finally told my boss the reason I'm taking vacation time, because I don't want him to find out accidentally. He immediately starts to panic thinking that I'll quit soon. That would be nice, but it's not financially possible. My boss says that he's going to run an ad in the paper to start getting candidates for my replacement. Is this a sign that it's time for me to quit? I really don't need this kind of stress right now.

Although the Society is making great strides in bringing the issue of expressing happiness to the public, we're far from being financially solvent.

✳

I fly from Dallas to California for the show. My brother, Michael, and my neighbor Kim, go with me, sort of. I'm on the official airline of the show, and they're on a different one. Of course, I get to fly first class, which is a real treat.

We reunite at the Los Angeles airport. A driver from the show picks us up. He drops us off at the hotel and tells us that someone will be back to pick us up for the taping the following afternoon.

At the hotel, *PI* has left a prep packet of possible show questions. I have wondered how each guest has something amusing, witty, or intelligent to say on every topic. Now I know; they get a cheat sheet.

The first question on the list is: "Pam Johnson, the founder of the Secret Society of Happy People, has announced August 8 as 'Admit You're Happy Day,' a day for people around the world to brush off their sorrows and own up to being happy. Is this necessary?"

The next three suggested questions are about Michelangelo's statue *David*. Also, men who feel discriminated against because they have to pay to place personal ads while women don't. And finally about baby boomers who can choose a new kind of funeral—celebratory roasts.

I spend the evening and the following day trying to think of possible smart aleck comments from Bill Maher and Richard Lewis. I also try to think of witty, yet truthful comebacks. By the time I arrive at the studio, I'm a nervous wreck. I try to remain cool on the outside, but I feel the future of the Society rests on my shoulders.

An escort takes us to the green room. It's small. Couches line the wall. A big TV is playing, so guests like my brother and Kim can watch the show while it's being taped. When we arrive, the green room is full of people. They are taping two shows, the one for tonight and my show for tomorrow night. I finally meet everyone I've been talking to over the phone for the past couple of months.

Dawn, a talent coordinator, introduces me to two other guests who will be on the show with me: actress Trina McGee-Davis and the Playboy Channel's Susannah Breslin. Scott, the producer, preps me for the show. I think it's his job to begin pitting the panelists against each other—makes for good entertainment. I don't meet Bill Maher, the host, beforehand. He's taping a show. I have also been forewarned that he likes the spontaneity of greeting guests while the cameras are rolling.

The panelists from the previous show come back to the green room. They hug, chat, and say good-bye to each other. It's time for us to tape.

I walk through the studio to the edge of the set. It is so much smaller than it looks on TV. I'll be the first guest introduced. I'm not going to kiss Bill Maher hello like lots of his guests do—after all I've never met the man. I hope and pray that I don't trip and fall when I'm walking out.

Bill does his intro skit. I know it's only a couple of minutes long, but it seems like forever. Finally he introduces me. I walk out and shake his hand. My hands are trembling and my heart is racing. I wonder if I look as scared as I feel. What if they say something and I can't come back with a funny response?

I sit in my chair. It's uncomfortable because my feet don't touch the ground. Don't they know some people are short?

Bill Maher introduces Susannah Breslin, the tallest woman I've ever seen in my life who dresses like an ad for Frederick's of Hollywood. Which makes sense, because she's a cybersex columnist and a correspondent for the Playboy Channel's *Sexetera*. Next, he introduces Trina McGee-Davis, who stars on the ABC sitcom *Boy Meets World*.

Finally, Bill introduces Richard Lewis, who's a frequent guest. I'm nervous because Richard is not only famous for being hopelessly neurotic and depressed, but also for his super-hyper delivery and for monopolizing every conversation.

Bill tries to open the topic of happiness by mentioning that it's Friday and many of the viewers spent the earlier part of the evening at happy hour.

Richard Lewis immediately jumps in and doesn't let Bill finish. Bill tries to get a word in, but Richard keeps jabbering away. Bill, again, tries to introduce the Secret Society of Happy People, but Richard is still interrupting and going off on tangents. Bill finally tells Richard to shut the *%^!#!* up (using a colorful expletive that was bleeped when the show aired).

I can't get a word in edgewise, but then neither can Bill, and he's the host. Finally, Bill gets in a sentence. He somewhat explains the Society's view that it's become politically incorrect and "not cool" to express happiness. I actually squeeze in a few sentences myself before Richard interrupts and goes off on his tangents again.

Trina is my ally. She tries to explain the Society's concept to Richard, who purposely pretends not to understand so he can do funny bits. Except the bits aren't really funny. Bill tries to rein in Richard, but it's no use.

Susannah is only slightly less annoying than Richard. She seems compelled to steer the conversation toward sex. She definitely does not like me. She says she thinks only people who are "slow in the head" can be happy. Everyone talks at once. Bill manages to comment on Susannah's observation. He ponders whether highly intelligent people are burdened by so much analytical thought that it's difficult for them to be happy. He cites a famous playwright as an example.

This could be interesting to discuss, but we don't get a chance because now Richard and Susannah are jabbering away at each other, a word here, a word there, half sentences, half thoughts. I'm not sure what to do.

Finally, Richard and I go back and forth about whether happy people are just denying pain—and everyone talks over each other again. Richard asks what my goal is, what do I expect from bringing the happiness issue to public attention via the Society.

Bill jumps in. To my relief, he says, "I think her thesis has a lot of merit."

Richard doesn't get it. How could he? He never lets anyone explain the concept. He continuously interrupts and misinterprets everything. During a commercial, he looks at me and says, "You know, this is just part of the shtick." Except that it's not entertaining and at this point the whole experience isn't even fun anymore.

Trina's and Bill's comments imply that they don't think Richard and Susannah's "shtick" is amusing either. This has ended my *Anything But Love* crush on Richard.

This first segment turns out to be a verbal feuding, a feeding frenzy. Susannah doesn't only steer every comment toward sex in general, she seems determined to talk about penises in particular. I'm as much a fan of penises as anyone, but this is ridiculous. She's speaking quite viciously to everyone.

It seems all the guests are frustrated and everyone but me has something bleeped when the show airs. I manage to make some comments about the misguided things Richard and Susannah keep repeating. Somehow, I am thinking pretty quickly on my feet, despite the fact that it's so out of control. I love *Politically Incorrect*, but I've never seen a segment quite like the one we're taping.

Richard and Susannah continue to discuss why highly paid, gorgeous models always look so unhappy. Trina asks Susannah what makes her happy. Susannah replies, "Penises."

I tell her there are a lot of men here (I look out at the audience) who have penises, so she should be very happy. I wonder whether this will all be bleeped when the show airs. I wonder if I'm going to need to explain to my mother that I actually had a good reason to say *penis* on national television. More than once.

Everyone argues whether or not Richard is happy. Richard says he's happy. Nobody believes him. I say that he might be happy, because he says he's happy. I try to give him the benefit of the doubt. Maybe his whole depressed, neurotic routine is just his act.

Well, apparently not. Bill says Richard's not happy, that he's known him for 20 years and in all that time he's never been happy. Richard corrects Bill, but not about happiness. He reminds Bill that they've actually known each other for 25 years. I tell Richard that I think he's very happy not being happy. Bill agrees; Richard is one of those people who are only happy when they're not happy, and that those kind of people are called New Yorkers.

This, of course, gets a very big laugh.

Next Bill talks about funerals and the latest trend of celebrations and roasts for the dearly departed. This leads to a big debate over grief and happiness. I have to point out the obvious. Everyone experiences loss; no one believes people can be happy all the time.

Richard says he'll bet that Susannah will be reincarnated as a penis. The audience laughs and applauds. I'm glad he gets the last laugh on Susannah's penis obsession.

After the next commercial, Bill says that since the word *penis* has already been so overused during the show, he'll bring up the evening's next scheduled topic. It's regarding a complaint by the father of a ten-year-old girl in Connecticut. Her school bus passes a replica of Michelangelo's famous—and naked—statue of David.

Susannah instantly complains that the statue is not well endowed enough; she's not impressed. Richard is finally fed up with Susannah.

He comes to the statue's defense, suggesting that perhaps David had just come out of the shower. Bill and Richard agree that it's a fine work of art, Susannah makes one more insane penis size reference, and we're out of time. That's it.

The show is over.

We line up for a photo. Richard runs over to stand between Trina and me. "I didn't want to be by the vixen," he says.

I return my microphone and walk to the green room. Unlike the last show's panel, I figure my gang won't be hugging and saying fond good-byes to each other. I'm right. They're all running out the door as I get back to the room. I feel a little shell shocked. I chat with Dawn, the talent coordinator, for a minute. Then, to my surprise, when I look out into the hall, Bill Maher is there. He looks at me and says, "You did a good job." I'm grateful for the kind remark.

After he leaves Dawn says, "He's never stopped by this green room before."

As we leave, my friend Kim is very supportive. She says I did a good job. She tells me that during the taping, the producers in the green room were surprised by how out of control the show got and how Bill was unable to explain the topic, because such a free-for-all ensued.

I still don't feel very good about the taping. My brother agrees with my assessment that I didn't do very well. I know he's right, but it would be nice if he would be a little less honest. Of course, he's the one who said he'd like to start the Society of Publicly Pissed-Off People. In all fairness, he's been supportive of the Society. He created the data-base and provides on-demand computer support services. Given that I can't even program my VCR, I call him often. Technology isn't exactly my forté.

We have to wait until the following night to see the show. It's going to be a long 24 hours. I feel like I'm in a dream. I knew it was happening, but it didn't seem real.

After we left the studio, I called my mother to tell her I used the word *penis* two times. She asks, "What does that have to do with happiness?" Of course, I immediately thought of several answers I don't want to discuss with my mother ever, but I explained that she'll understand when she sees the show. I'm just warning her ahead of time.

I watch the show on Friday night while we're still in California. To my surprise it doesn't come across as awful as it felt at the time. They must have edited out some of the overlapping conversation, so you could actually hear one person at a time. Even as broadcast, the show was still a free-for-all. After watching it though, I feel better. My brother even agrees that the broadcast didn't have the same tumultuous feeling as the taping. Kim smiles and says in a nonchalant tone, "I told you that you did a good job." This is the first time I can remember hearing an "I told you so" that was good.

The Society gets a lot of messages of support. Several people post notes on the happy board (they weren't fond of Richard and Susannah).

After I get back from California, I try to reflect on this experience. I keep asking myself the same question: Do I ever want to do this again? All I'm trying to do is encourage people to talk about being happy—if they happen to be happy. The Society doesn't tell anyone to be happy or how to be happy. We have a neutral message. Why do people make it so convoluted?

It's almost as if people perceive happiness as a weakness.

Then I started to think about human nature. We are, after all, just animals. All animals have their number one priority: their own survival. And that means minimizing their weaknesses and fortifying their strengths.

When you are nice, when you are open, or when you display joy or happiness, you are vulnerable to the reactions of other people. If they choose to attack your positive actions or mood, you could feel hurt or disappointed.

When you are nice, when you are open, or when you display joy or happiness, you are by definition not taking a hostile or aggressive stance. You're not attacking someone, and you're not protecting yourself either. Again, you are left vulnerable.

Is it any wonder that people are wary of expressing happiness? Cranky characters in predatory moods love to interpret happiness as a weakness and then attack. What's a happy person to do?

In *The Seven Spiritual Laws of Success*, Deepak Chopra notes that people spend 99 percent of their time defending their points of view. Closely tied to that is the habit we have of thinking we should share all of our thoughts, news, or desires with everyone. "Keep your desires to yourself," Chopra writes. "Do not share them with anyone else unless they share the exact same desires that you have and are closely bonded with you."

If you want to cut back on the number of negative responses you get to your positive outlook, maybe part of the solution is to be pickier about who you can open up to about those things.

Although the advice makes sense on a practical level, I still think the solution is to get people talking about happiness again. When more people do, it will become the norm and people won't be as anxious to rain on other people's parades.

But until the philosophy of "When You're Happy and You Know It...Tell Someone" is more accepted, and if you know you are in the company of "parade-rainers," maybe it's better to just share your happiness nonverbally. You can express it through the twinkle in your eye or the smile on your face. Just keep 'em guessing.

Now that the trip and the taping are behind me, I have time to focus on National Admit You're Happy Day—August 8. I picked that date because it marks the Society's first full year. That's the day when we got our first member. It's our birthday.

I decide to ask the governor of every state to send us a proclamation naming August 8 National Admit You're Happy Day. It should be fun. I'm sure that all the governors will want to participate. After all, how often can they issue a bipartisan, nonpolitical proclamation that has a positive impact on at least 99 percent of their citizens? Most people have had at least one happy moment.

Immediately we send letters requesting our proclamations. That gives the governors four months to process them. Who's going to say no? Which one will we get first?

April 1999

Scatter seeds of kindness everywhere you go;
scatter bits of courtesy—watch them grow and grow.
Gather buds of friendship; keep them till full-blown;
you will find more happiness than you have ever known.

Amy R. Raabe

This is my first break since the end of November. The seeds we've planted are taking root. The Society continues to get mentioned in stories, but it's just one here and there—not everywhere at once.

I finally convinced my boss that I'm not leaving my full-time job—I might want to, but I can't afford it. It still remains a real time challenge to get the Society's message out while I continue working because I'm required to travel so much.

I love the Society because it gives me a chance to help spread a little cheer and deliver a serious message that happiness needs to be expressed more.

I've recovered from the shell shock of being on *PI*. Hindsight being 20/20 I realize that although the show turned into a free-for-all, it proves that people are uncomfortable with the idea of simply expressing happiness. And more important, Bill Maher understood and supported the idea of the Society. So how do I get booked on the show again?

The *Glamour* magazine sidebar runs. It was a perfect one-liner about the Society.

I'm shocked and disappointed because the governors'offices are sending rejection letters for our proclamation request for National

Admit You're Happy Day. Most claim that a citizen of their state or a local sponsor, must request a proclamation, but that's not a problem since we have members in most states. My goal is to have a proclamation from all 50 states. I'll just have to get those local sponsors.

May 1999

Happiness always looks small
while you hold it in your hands,
But let it go,and you can learn at once
how big and precious it is.

Maxim Gorky

The daytime TV season is almost over. They'll be going on summer hiatus soon. We haven't been booked on any other shows yet. I'm a little disappointed. Our message is empowering. It gives people permission to be happy and express it. Maybe the daytime shows don't see the Society as fitting in with their usual fare.

I start calling the governors' offices to find out the status of our proclamation requests. Many of them haven't received the request (so they claim). Others require local sponsors, and some won't decide until July.

Everyone requests a sample proclamation. If they don't know what one should say, how would I know what it should say? A couple of offices are kind enough to send me samples.

We wrote the following sample proclamation:

SAMPLE PROCLAMATION FOR

NATIONAL ADMIT YOU'RE HAPPY DAY

August 8th, 1999

WHEREAS, In August 1998, the Secret Society of Happy People was formed to encourage people of all ages and backgrounds to talk more about their happy events and moments: and

WHEREAS, the Secret Society of Happy People serves as the consumer advocate for a person's right to express happiness by discouraging people from raining on other people's parades: and

WHEREAS, National Admit You're Happy Day and the entire month of August is designated to encourage the citizens of (your state) and beyond to talk about happiness with their families, friends, co-workers, and even strangers: and

WHEREAS, (Your state) State government has a responsibility to encourage it's citizens to reflect on the happiness in their lives and to help improve the quality of that expression in conversations with families, friends, and others:

NOW, THEREFORE, I, (Governor's Name), GOVERNOR OF THE STATE OF (your state), do hereby proclaim August 8th, 1999 and the month of August as

National Admit You're Happy Day

and urge all (your state) citizens to acknowledge and to further their commitment to talking about the happy events and moments in their lives.

June 1999

*The happiest person is the person
who thinks the most interesting thoughts.*

William Lyon Phelps

I recruited Society members to be local sponsors in the states that required them. It's fun talking to them. I prepared and sent packets requesting the proclamations to the sponsors. They'll sign the request letter and forward the packet to their state governors. I hope there's still time to get them through the government bureaucracy.

We're also going to get America to vote on the Top Ten Happiest Events, Inventions and Social Changes of the Century. People can vote on our web site or by mail-in ballot. I hope a few newspapers will print the ballot so their readers can vote. We want people of all ages to participate. I imagine families, friends, and co-workers discussing and debating the ballots with each other. It'll be just one way to encourage happy conversations.

I request nominations for the list through an e-mail. Voting will begin in August and finish at the end of September. That way there will be time for schools to vote and for mail-in ballots to be returned. I start to get the ballots ready. I send out the advance press releases naming August 8, 1999, the very first National Admit You're Happy Day.

Since we couldn't have a convention for National Admit You're Happy Day this first year, we're going to have a party at my apartment complex clubhouse. Maybe next year, we'll get to have that convention.

July 1999

The U.S. Constitution doesn't guarantee happiness,
Only the pursuit of it.
You have to catch up with it yourself.

Benjamin Franklin

The press coverage for National Admit You're Happy Day, that I had hoped would begin in August, hit a column in the *San Francisco Chronicle* on July 2. The publicity ball is rolling again. It's early, fast, and furious.

After the *San Francisco Chronicle* story was printed, I receive a call from the *Dallas Morning News*. They want to do a story and they want it now. Other newspapers print excerpts from the *San Francisco Chronicle* column, so we start getting e-mail from people who want to vote for the Happiest Events, Inventions and Social Changes of the Century. I had planned to put these on-line in August, not July! So it's not on my webmaster's schedule until the end of the month. Why didn't I learn more about computers when I was in college?

I'm excited and grateful for the coverage, but I'm just not ready to respond this early. It wasn't part of the plan, but then nothing about the Society has followed a plan. Why would it start being predictable now? If everyone is writing about us now, will they still cover the actual day, August 8?

This early coverage led a reporter from *People* to call.

We start getting a lot of calls from single men who are looking for single "happy" women. I sometimes think if I had set up the Secret Society of Happy People Dating Service, I'd be able to fund the Secret Society of Happy Kids' nonprofit organization.

✳

In the midst of this, I call the governors' offices almost daily. Their aides are finally figuring it out: I'm not going to go away. They just don't like to return phone calls.

The good news is that a handful of governors' offices give us a quick and easy yes. Cheers to Nebraska, Washington, and Colorado.

I have to accept that since we don't have local sponsors in all states, we're not going to get proclamations from all of them. I decide to create a special category for these states: the "Sticks in the Mud" Governors. Since happiness is universal and the expression of it is important, I think they should have made an exception for this proclamation.

Most of the gubernatorial offices are still debating our request. Here are some of the responses from the governors' aides:

Oklahoma

From Frank Keating's office: "I'm not sure this should be a National Day. But we'll send the request to the legal department."

Why would a day to admit you're happy need to be reviewed by the legal department? I call back after a couple of weeks and get the same response. It's not like we are suggesting a "Take Your Gun to Work Day." On second thought, if we were, we might be better received because we'd be viewed as potential campaign contributors.

Minnesota

From Jesse Ventura's office: "Governor Ventura represents the citizens of Minnesota and doesn't see how this impacts them."

How could happiness not impact the citizens of Minnesota?

New York

I call Governor George E. Pataki's office, and explain my request for a proclamation for National Admit You're Happy Day to an aide. She puts me on hold and when she returns, she announces, "We have no official position." I assume that she just picked up the wrong line. I immediately re-explain the reason for my call.

Again, she responds, "We have no official position on happiness. We're waiting to see what the other governors and the federal government does. We'll know on August 7."

At this point I laugh to myself, especially since August 7 is a Saturday. I can't imagine a governor going to work that day to make a decision about my little proclamation. I say to the aide, "Some of the governors are giving us proclamations and others aren't. That's why we're calling, to see what your office is going to do. We didn't ask the federal government for a proclamation so they aren't doing anything."

The aide is frustrated. She ends the conversation by repeating, "We have no official position."

This whole conversation left me speechless (if that's possible). I can't believe it's been so much trouble to get proclamations. My dream of issuing a press release with a headline that reads "All 50 governors declare August 8 as National Admit You're Happy Day" is over. For some reason, it was clear, they weren't sure what to do about this day. I guess no one has ever asked the governors their position on a person's right to express happiness. Maybe the Society should start.

A couple of friends tell me these responses are so funny that we should issue a press release. I'm not sure about that. They were funny, but would it be nice to issue a press release about these responses? One friend reminds me the governors' offices aren't being nice. Our release would just point out the strange reaction people have when you ask them to encourage the expression of happiness. It's as if the governors' offices are in a serious debate: "Do we want our citizens to talk about happiness or keep it to themselves? What should we do?" If the Society issues the press release, will it encourage some undecided governors to participate or at least respond to our request?

By now, other newspapers are interviewing us for stories about National Admit You're Happy Day. I share the governors' responses with several reporters, including the *Washington Post*, the *San Diego Tribune*, and *People* magazine. The reporters think the responses are funny, so I go ahead and issue a press release. The Associated Press picked up the story and it went on the national wire just in time for the Monday morning news.

I start doing radio interviews by phone Monday morning and after each one, I have several phone messages to return. One is from CNN: "Can you be in a field studio at 1:00 P.M.?" I say yes.

It's very hectic. Fortunately my mom is in town visiting and helps me keep up with my messages.

Tuesday, I'm scheduled to go out of town for a conference for my day job. I can't miss it. So for the entire week I schedule interviews around my business schedule. Reporters agree to call me at the hotel.

The Associated Press story is great, but it has an error. The reporter mistakenly says I'd received a letter from Pataki's office. There was no letter and I never said there was. The exchange with Governor Pataki's aide was a phone conversation. The fact that the aide told me that Pataki had "no official position" on happiness numerous times, is what made it funny. Of course, Pataki's office wasn't amused by our press release or the AP story. They keep saying they didn't send a letter. Which they didn't. Nor did I claim that they did. They don't deny the aide's comment, but they say she is not in a position to be an official spokesperson. How could I have known that?

The problem should be solved with a simple correction by the Associated Press. Just say the reporter made a mistake. But that's not what happens. The correction sounds like I lied and said there was a letter when there wasn't. I am devastated. This is my personal credibility being questioned. Why isn't the AP being fair in their correction?

I called the AP offices in Dallas and New York to try to have them issue a correction to the correction. They refuse. The Dallas office goes so far as to tell me they've given the Society enough publicity and won't cover us again. We'd have to get our message out through other sources.

I am shocked and mortified. I feel so powerless. After all, do they refuse to cover the high-tech industry or the latest kid trend because they've already given them enough coverage? The reality is that when the AP doesn't pick up your story, millions of people who would have enjoyed reading it or hearing about it won't get to. No other organization can contact all of the print and broadcast outlets individually— the AP is crucial for worldwide coverage.

Our press releases aren't just about getting coverage for the

Society. They're interesting and newsworthy, and have a goal, to get people to talk about happiness. It's unfair that I'm personally being made to look bad for trying to do a good thing. All I could think of was, "What's wrong with this picture?"

As this unfolds, I'm still out of town. I'm working a conference for my day job while I'm doing all the publicity for the Society. I am on the phone doing radio interviews and speaking with print reporters almost every hour between 6:00 A.M. and 10:00 P.M. Then I have to answer all of the e-mails the Society is getting.

Most of the radio interviews are fun, but I always have to clarify that the Society isn't telling people to "be happy." I start reminding reporters of a scene in *Steel Magnolias*, where Shirley MacLaine, who's normally chronically cranky, goes to Dolly Parton's beauty salon in a surprisingly chipper mood. Julia Roberts's character had done a little matchmaking for her. Julia comments that Shirley is in particularly good spirits. "I'm a happy person," Shirley says. "I've just been in a bad mood for forty years."

The message of the Society is that even if you've been in a bad mood for forty years, but you happen to have a happy moment, you have a right to express it without people raining on your parade. The reporters laugh.

One talk radio host who was promoting my interview while I was on hold listening to the show, said on-air, "There's a woman from Plano, who drives a Mercedes, has a pool and is married to a rich man who wants you to be happy on August 8." None of this is true. For the record, I do not live in the Dallas suburb of Plano. I don't drive a Mercedes or any other luxury car. I live in an apartment. I'm not married, and never have been. I'm not wealthy. And, no, I don't have a rich Sugar Daddy, either.

Other reporters think I'm part of a Christian group or affiliated with some other religious organization. I'm not. The Society attracts people from all religions because happiness is a common feeling that can bring people together. And of course, I'm always asked "Are you happy all of the time?"

The week becomes a blur. I am going to bed in tears from exhaustion. I want to be home. I get to go home on Friday, but I'm traveling again on business from Sunday through Tuesday.

Our party for Admit You're Happy Day is set for the following

Saturday. Sunday will be National Admit You're Happy Day. The AP coverage helps us get a few more proclamations. It's interesting to see how fast governors' offices respond when they get calls from the local newspapers.

I finally get home for the weekend, I immediately write letters to newspaper editors across the country for their OP-ED pages, telling my side of the story about the AP incident. I just want the editors to know the error was the AP reporter's, not mine. I also have to return phone calls, answer e-mails, mail, and send faxes. We still have governors who are undecided about our proclamation.

I have moments that I wonder what I've created and if it is worth the effort. I know that the message of the Society benefits people. But the incident with the AP questions my personal credibility. The radio interviewers want me to make their listeners happy. I am constantly explaining that the Society doesn't make people happy unless someone happens to think we're amusing. Some DJs just don't like us. Memberships aren't paying the Society's high expenses.

In the final analysis, I realize I'm being personally attacked for encouraging people to express something as innocent as happiness, and it's costing me a lot of money.

We are also getting a lot of unhappy postings on the web site's happy board. My web master is having a hard time keeping up with the removal of inappropriate messages—the ones you definitely don't want your kids to read.

I talk to a couple of friends about the Society's future. I ask if they think I should continue. I'm just not sure the message is worth the effort, emotional drain, and financial cost. I know I need to get through National Admit You're Happy Day. I need to send out another newsletter, but after that, I'm just not sure whether to continue.

I speak to my mom about my frustrations. She immediately understands that I am way too tired to make any decisions. "The message of the Society is just getting out," she says. "If you quit now, you'll regret it. Just get through National Admit You're Happy Day, and then get some rest before you decide."

I know she's right, but I'm busy feeling sorry for myself. The AP incident is more than I can take. I've been blackballed from coverage for no reason. It isn't fair. This whole thing just isn't going as planned. At this moment, I'm not having fun. And, no, I'm not happy.

I have one more chaotic week ahead of me, then I can get a little rest and perspective so I can make decisions.

The exciting news is that the governors' proclamations are starting to arrive. Some are so beautiful, and they are all exciting to get. I receive an e-mail from a man who's seen the press coverage regarding the governors' responses to National Admit You're Happy Day. He's read the unhappy news that government is threatened by celebrating happiness. He believes there are obvious reasons for this: Government is a business that aims to solve problems, he says, but if people feel happy (and aren't focused on their problems), government goes "out of business." He also writes that jealousy is a factor too. People resent those who are happy. And finally, he notes, medical researchers believe that our ability to be happy is so affected by our brain chemicals and their balance that some people quite literally aren't biologically capable of being happy. He wonders if that includes some governors.

Another e-mail moves me as well. The writer is a teenage girl, who just read about the Society in the newspaper and then visited our web site. She says that it made her think about how often she finds herself thinking like "a grouch." All too often, she says, she talks about how she'd like to lose a few pounds or have more money, or she complains about "millions of other tiny things." Now, she says, after reading the web site, "I realize I need to just shut up about all that crap and focus on all the great things I have in my life." She cites her family, friends, home, good health, good grades at school, sports accomplishments, and "a bright future." She says, "I'm going to stop making myself miserable by comparing myself to other people, and, instead, I'm going to start living."

If only every teenager could come to that same conclusion. If only our culture didn't play on their insecurities for profit. If only adults would set the example.

When I get these types of messages they re-affirm the need for the Secret Society of Happy People. I know with all my heart and soul that the Society's message is having a positive impact on thousands, if not millions of people. This makes me very happy and all my aggravation and frustration vanish. After all they were only moments.

August 1999

*Even if happiness forgets you a little bit,
never completely forget it.*

Jacques PrEvert

Several of the local proclamation sponsors have called and e-mailed me to find out what their own governor did about our proclamation requests. Some are actually calling their governors' offices themselves to find out. Reporters are calling me to get final tallies. I wish the governors' offices would be a little more cooperative. It's not like this should be controversial. Why wouldn't they want their citizens to express happiness?

Other responses that arrived this week are

Florida

Governor Jeb Bush sends me an e-mail that says:

"As we approach National Admit You're Happy Day, I am writing on two counts. First to say that as a rule we don't do resolutions such as these and, secondly, to tell you that I admit I am happy most of the time. I count my blessings for the good things in my life and encourage others to do the same."

I respond:

"Thanks for the reply. I'm sure our members in Florida will be disappointed that you didn't issue a proclamation for National Admit You're Happy Day. Although you will be on the Parade-

Raining Governors List, I'm happy to report that when you're happy you openly admit it and encourage others to do so."

His final response was: "No rain here in the Sunshine state."

The irony here is that he supports the message, we have a local sponsor, and he still doesn't give us a proclamation.

Michigan

An aide in Governor John Engler's office responds, "We've already issued the proclamations for August and don't want to lessen the importance of them."

Now how could any proclamation be more important than one that encourages their citizens to talk about happiness? And how could supporting the expression of happiness lessen the importance of other proclamations? Whatever happened to our government's support of the right to "the pursuit of happiness"? Oh, that's the problem: They support the pursuit but not the expression.

Georgia

An aide in Governor Roy Barnes's office replies, "We don't give national proclamations unless the president of the United States issues them for things like National Boating Week."

The only thing I can think of is that what they really are saying is that I need PAC money to get proclamations for happiness.

Missouri

Governor Mel Carnahan's office: Originally in July his office had said they would give us a proclamation, but then they changed their mind (but wouldn't give a reason).

They didn't send a proclamation. Why would you change your mind about the expression of happiness?

By the time everything was said and done (October 1, 1999), our official results were:

Happy Governors
Proclaimed August 8
National Admit You're Happy Day

Alabama—Don Siegelman
Connecticut—John G. Rowland
Idaho—Dirk Kempthorne
Indiana—Frank O'Bannon
Iowa—Tom Vilsack
Maryland—Parris N. Glendening
Massachusetts—Argeo Paul Cellucci
Nebraska—Mike Johanns
Nevada—Kenny C. Guinn
New Hampshire—Jeanne Shaheen
New Jersey—Christine T. Whitman
North Carolina—James B. Hunt Jr.
Oregon—John A. Kitzhaber
Rhode Island—Lincoln Almond
Texas—George W. Bush
Vermont—Howard Dean, M.D.
Washington—Gary Locke
West Virginia—Cecil H. Underwood
Wisconsin—Tommy G. Thompson

Stick in the Mud
Wouldn't give us a proclamation
because we didn't meet state
guidelines

Alaska—Tony Knowles
Arkansas—Mike Huckabee
Delaware—Thomas R. Carper
Hawaii—Benjamin J. Cayetano
Kentucky—Paul E. Patton
North Dakota—Edward T. Schafer
South Dakota—William J. Janklow

Parade-Raining Governors
Wouldn't give us a proclamation

Arizona—Jane Dee Hull
Florida—Jeb Bush
Georgia—Roy Barnes
Illinois—George H. Ryan
Kansas—Bill Graves
Louisiana—Mike Foster
Maine—Angus S. King Jr.
Michigan—John Engler
Minnesota—Jesse Ventura
Mississippi—Kirk Fordice
Missouri—Mel Carnahan
Montana—Marc Racicot
New Mexico—Gary E. Johnson
Ohio—Bob Taft
Pennsylvania—Tom Ridge
South Carolina—Jim Hodges
Tennessee—Don Sundquist
Virginia—James S. Gilmore III
Wyoming—Jim Geringer

Beyond Words
Sent a proclamation for
National Admit Your Hapy Day
and took it back in September

Colorado—Bill Owens

No Official Position

New York—George E. Pataki

No Response

California—Gray Davis
Oklahoma—Frank Keating
Utah—Michael O. Leavitt

✳

I return from my business trip on Tuesday in time to finish organizing the National Admit You're Happy Day party we're having Saturday. I hope we'll get some national TV coverage; however, we've had so much prepublicity, it doesn't seem that we going to get much coverage the actual day of the event.

A Dallas radio station, *KISS-FM*, is coming to the party, Clinique's Happy Fragrances sent prizes for the participants, and DJ.com put together an hour of happy music.

On Thursday, I receive a call from the photo department of *People* magazine. They want to send a photographer to the party. Since I haven't heard from the reporter I had spoke with earlier, I'm surprised to get this phone call. Not only do they want to send a photographer to the party, they also want to shoot some candid photos on Saturday.

The following week they'll send another photographer to take more photos. Their initial suggestion was to show me having car problems and being happy about it. This is not the message of the Society. I immediately send them alternative ideas for photos that better represent the message of the Society.

I speak with the first photographer who'll be doing Saturday's shoot. He wants to photograph me "doing something happy." We agree on roller blading. He asks if I could have some friends roller blade with me. It's Friday afternoon. Most of my friends are coming to the party tomorrow and I'm not sure they can also show up for a photo shoot before it.

The photographer comes Saturday afternoon and my friend Annie, who has only roller bladed once, agrees to roller blade with me. He shoots the photos and will be back that evening for the party.

My Aunt Barbara and several friends help me put the party together. They pick up food, put it out, serve beverages, and help decorate. I couldn't have done it without them. Society members from the Dallas area and even a few from out of town attend the party. I'm relieved to see them all there.

I also had invited my apartment complex neighbors. To my surprise, the complex office received a call from a resident who wants to know if the Secret Society of Happy People was just a code name or clever euphemism for a "gay" party. Will I ever get over being shocked at the questions we get?

The party goes well. National Admit You're Happy Day is relatively quiet so I get to rest, which makes me very happy.

Stories run all weekend. Of course, when you receive national press you not only get messages from people who like you but also from those who don't like you. I sometimes think these people are in the middle of a personal rainstorm and are desperately trying to find the rainbow. I only wish I could show it to them.

The only thing that I overlooked in planning National Admit You're Happy Day was the fact that we're an international organization. We inadvertently made our international members unhappy. So next year it'll just be Admit You're Happy Day.

I spend the early part of the week getting stuff lined up for the second *People* photo shoot, it's on Wednesday. I have to organize friends for a photo that I don't want taken. *People* wants me wearing a bright color with lots of people dressed in black around me. Of course, I had to find the people and this visual didn't capture the message of the Society. I had proposed something with rain gear and umbrellas for the "Don't rain on my parade" theme. I also suggested something funny with the 100 Happiest Events, Inventions, and Social Changes of the Century list. To my relief they agreed to those poses too. I hope they'll be the ones that get printed.

The *People* reporter comes to my house to interview me. In the middle of all this, the *Houston Chronicle* decides to do a story and also sends a photographer. I'm beginning to get a new respect for models. To my surprise, smiling naturally on command can be challenging.

In my wildest dreams, I never guessed that I'd be the center of all the publicity. I really want the message to be about the Society and not me. For now though I seem to be the media spokesperson to spread the message.

I receive an envelope in the mail from the *St. Charles Gazette*, a West Virginia newspaper. They've run an article about our century list. The graphics are really cute and they've printed our list of 100 items to be voted on. I can't wait to read the story but when I do, my excitement quickly dissipates. The story presents the list as if the Society were telling you that these things will make you happy. They forgot the "in this century" part. I had to again send a letter to the editor telling our side of the story. I feel like I'm being placed on the defensive about the expression of happiness. It seems ludicrous that something so simple is constantly misunderstood.

Several newspapers printed the 100 item ballot, so people are mailing them in. Votes are also coming in via the internet. This also means people are complaining about what's on the list. Why isn't love and spending time with your family on the list? I politely write back that those things aren't new to this century.

We decide to update the web site. I made the difficult choice to take down the Happy Board. I hope to bring it back some day; but some people use the happy board to be mean and verbally abusive. That creates a lot of unhappiness, and that's not the purpose of our web site.

The *People* magazine story is scheduled for the August 29 issue, which means it will hit the newsstands sometime after August 22. When the reporter called to do a fact check, there were several errors. I have no idea which picture they've chosen or how the final copy will read. It's nerve-wracking waiting to see how they'll tell our story. If they misrepresent the mission of the Society, this could be the beginning of the end.

I still haven't had time to slow down and think about the next direction for the Society. It's as if a force greater than myself is guiding this mission and I'm just a messenger. Perhaps that's why I don't have time to think. I only have time to listen to my gut and do.

I start writing a business plan to get a Small Business Administration (SBA) secured loan so I can order and sell merchandise with funny slogans that represent the message of the Society. We keep getting requests for T-shirts, buttons, coffee mugs, and other fun stuff all the time. Some people like the message of the Society but don't want to be "members." The first two slogans I chose are "Don't Even Think of Raining on My Parade" and "When You're Happy and You Know It...Tell Someone."

The banks says there's a problem with my loan application: We're not asking for enough money. They prefer business loans of at least

$75,000 because they believe they are more cost effective to process. Our business plan is for only $48,000. We finally get three banks to process the loan application, so now I just have to wait. I hope we receive the loan by the beginning of October, so we can offer some happy products in time for the holiday gift season.

The *People* story comes out and I'm jubilant. My worries were for nothing. The article is accurate and funny. They use my rain gear photo idea: I'm sitting under an umbrella as my friend Melissa pours water over it, trying to "rain on my parade," as it were. The magazine's photo department tells me that they loved the happiest items of the century photo, but that wasn't mentioned in the story. That's a pity, because lots of people don't know they can still vote. Again, we are inundated with e-mails even though the *People* story doesn't list our web site. Some people join the Society, but mostly we get messages like, "glad you're doing this, someone needs to."

All of this publicity has prompted several people to contact us about starting local chapters, including one girl in high school. This is heartwarming and offers great promise for the future. The seeds of our efforts are just beginning to sprout.

I wonder where we'll be next year?

The happy possibilities are endless.

September 1999

Let us be grateful to people who make us happy;
they are the charming gardeners who make our souls blossom.

Marcel Proust

I love the shelf life of magazines, because we're still getting responses from the *People* story.

The Society receives e-mails daily, but I get one that stands out because it clearly expresses what so many others I've received from men and women of all ages, all backgrounds, all kinds of professions (even the military!) have. But this one is from a teenage boy who writes that he has been described as "disgustingly perky," "too happy," and therefore "stupid" and "immature" for sharing his happiness with his classmates and adults. He says he greets adults with a smile and asks, "How are you?" There was a time this kind of behavior was the ideal, but times have changed, and not for the better. He says, adults respond to his pleasantries by reacting as if he's being "a pest," or "a smart-ass," or even "disrespectful." When he remarks that it's a nice day, some people respond by giving him a look "like I should be committed," he writes. He has come to the conclusion that being positive and happy has become "politically incorrect."

Back in February, I received an e-mail from a male Army officer, who wrote that he's often accused of being "too casual" or "lacking a sense of urgency" because he has a happy and optimistic nature. Though he's successful, he says he's been told that he'd be more successful if he "wasn't as happy." And then he writes, "Isn't that twisted?" He says professionally, his optimistic nature is misconstrued as "lacking seriousness." He reminds us all that even serious matters are easier to deal with "when everyone is in great spirits."

Another man e-mails us that he isn't "taken as seriously" as his colleagues who scowl and bemoan how bad everything is. In the business world, he says, promotions are based on pessimism instead of optimism. "We are accused of being Pollyannas who can't see that Big Problem," he says.

A woman e-mails in saying she thinks she lost her previous job for "being too happy." The owner of the business said she didn't take her job seriously enough because she was "always cheerful, even in a crisis." Now, she writes, she works in a terrific place where the people are upbeat and have a sense of humor, like her.

The three banks I contacted have all said no to my loan request, so I have to complete another application. I'm getting discouraged, but I've been told persistence is the key to success. The applications are long and cumbersome, and the back-up materials take forever to put together. The funny part is that it's all a guess anyway. It's not like there's a tried-and-true formula that guarantees any business will succeed; but at least we've consistently gotten a ton of press during the past year and people are interested in our message. That means, I think, that our T-shirts, bumper stickers, and other happy stuff should sell just fine.

The loan officer at the fourth bank likes our idea. She thinks she can get it approved. When it comes back, I'm told they'll fund the loan if I go through the prequalification program at the SBA. Why didn't they tell me this at the beginning? This just created at least another thirty-day delay. I need approval now, not next month. What am I going to do?

Grudgingly, I assemble all the paperwork for the prequalification program at the SBA. Now I just have to wait to get my response. My patience is running out.

So many possibilities, so many obstacles, but the dream is alive and becoming a reality.

At last, I give notice at my day job. I tell my boss I'm leaving the first of October. I can't possibly continue to do stuff for the Society and meet the requirements of this job. There's way too much travel, and I'm not being fair to the job or the Society. So, I'm going to invest my life's savings in the Society and I'll probably have to get a part-time job. I'm working on a program that companies and wellness centers can implement to encourage the expression of happiness. Plans are also underway for a nonprofit organization, the Secret Society of Happy Kids.

I send new possible show ideas to some of the daytime talk shows. I hope we get responses. I know audiences would find us amusing, enlightening, and empowering

An aide from Colorado Governor Owens's office calls me on September 27 and says they want their proclamation back! I ask, "Why?"

The woman on the phone explains, "We didn't mean to issue it."

"Please send me a memo requesting that I return the proclamation," I say formally. I learned my lesson about not having back up proof in print back in July. I can't believe this conversation. Why would someone ask for a proclamation back? Is it even possible to take something back after it already happened? I feel like I just entered the Twilight Zone. Will I ever wake up?

People are enjoying voting on the Happiest Events, Inventions, and Social Changes of the Century and we're still getting ballots in by mail. I wonder what will be the happiest event, invention, or social change of the century.

I received a note in the mail from a woman who says she took our Top 100 Century voting ballot with her when she went to visit her seventy-two-year-old sister, who is dying. The woman, her sister, and five other family members spent an enjoyable hour discussing their choices, she says, and forgetting all about the sister's illness.

When I read notes like this, I know that all the hassles are worth it. Forget about the grumpy people who give us a hard time. The Society was created in the first place to represent people like this woman.

October 1999

*Happiness does not come from doing easy work
but from the afterglow of satisfaction
that comes after the achievement of a difficult task
that demanded our best.*

Theodore I. Rubin

Jim, the counselor coordinator from the Small Business Development Center (SBDC), who's been helping me with my SBA prequalification application and business plan called. He says my application is being sent through the legal department because of the words "Secret Society". They're concerned that we might be a neo-Nazi group. I'm not only shocked but insulted. Have they even taken the time to read any of the material in the application, or the press coverage? Did they look at our logo or visit our web site?

Our members are from every race and ethnic group in the United States and abroad. As one Society volunteer points out, most of the people who've helped put the logistics of the Society together, including my editor and current web designer, are Jewish. This is crazy. And, again, it's slowing down the loan process.

I order smaller amounts of merchandise than I want and start putting together the next issue of our newsletter and catalog. It has to go into the mail in November, loan or no loan.

I also tabulate the 10,000 votes we received and issue the results of the 100 Happiest Events, Inventions, and Social Changes of the Century.

The Happiest
Events, Inventions, and Social Changes
of the Century

1. Indoor plumbing
2. Air conditioning
3. Medical technology—procedures, vaccines, and cures
4. Women's right to vote
5. Washers and Dryers
6. Television
7. The internet
8. E-mail
9. Personal health products—Band-Aids, deodorant, toothpaste, and so on
10. PCs
11. Radio
12. Phones—cordless and cell
13. Microwaves
14. Margaret Sanger for legalizing birth control
15. The Civil Rights Act
16. Women wearing pants and choosing hemlines
17. Man walking on the moon in 1969
18. Motorized cars
19. Movies with sound
20. Social Security
21. Contact lenses
22. Dr. Seuss
23. Wright brothers airplane—1904
24. CD players
25. Remote control*
25. Active fathers*
26. Paved roads
27. Dishwashers
28. Call Waiting, Three-Way Calling, Caller I-D, Conference Calling
29. Pizza delivery
30. *The Far Side*
31. Sunglasses
32. VCRs and video cameras
33. The Beatles
34. *Winnie the Pooh*
35. Disney empire*
35. Cable TV*
36. Self-adhesive stamps
37. Celebration of cultural diversity
38. Post-Its
39. Personal cameras
40. *Sesame Street*
41. *The Wizard of Oz*
42. Answering machines
43. *Star Wars*
44. Girl Scout cookies
45. Wal-Mart

46. NASA
47. Indoor malls
48. McDonald's
49. Blow dryers
50. Mother's Day*
50. *Captain Kangaroo*
51. Affordable long distance
52. Elvis Presley
53. Satellites*
53. Hair dye*
54. The '57 Chevy**
54. Sneakers**
54. Business Casual**
55. Kool-Aid
56. Woodstock
57. Super Bowl
58. Father's Day*
58. White-Out*
59. Model T-Ford**
59. Mass production**
60. Automatic drip coffee-maker*
60. Stand up comics*
61. *Peanuts***
61. *Dilbert***
62. Flower children*
62. John Deere tractors*
62. The World Series*

63. Power lawn mowers**
63. Pagers**
63. Macy's Thanksgiving Day Parade**
64. The 1976 Bicentennial Celebration*
64. Phonograph*
65. *Gone with the Wind*
66. Helicopters
67. Rural Electric Coop
68. Acrylic nails*
68. Hula hoops*
69. Video Arcades
70. Barbie and GI Joe
71. Electric typewriters
72. *New Year's Eve in Times Square with Dick Clark*
72. *The Ed Sullivan Show*
73. Tanning booths**
73. Roller blades**
73. Jukebox**
74. TV dinners*
74. Dry cleaning*
75. Federal Express
76. Cosmetic surgery
77. Wall-to-wall carpeting
78. Mood rings
79. Electric razors
80. Buses

* / ** These items were tied with the items above or below them. (Because of the ties there are only 80 places but 100 items.)

To my delight everything got a vote. The fact that indoor plumbing won both the internet and mail-in ballots surprises me a little. I suppose I just thought the internet voters would take indoor plumbing for granted, since most of them never lived without it. But I guess everyone appreciates the simple things the most.

Our press release included a funny picture of me at an outhouse. Several newspapers including the *Dallas Morning News* ran this story and more papers picked it up. We haven't been bombarded by radio interviews since we're still being black-listed by the Associated Press. Of course, this list would have been fun for radio. I'm sad that listeners missed out because the AP won't judge the Society's press releases based on their newsworthiness anymore. I don't know what to do to correct the situation. All I know is that our press releases aren't being objectively reviewed, because they're worried about giving "happiness" or "the Society" too much coverage. Have they forgotten that news is more than money, crime, disaster, and corruption?

✳

I check my messages and there's one from the man at the SBA who must approve my request for the prequalification letter I need to get my loan.

I return his call and he asks me if the Society discriminates against anyone. I reply, "Maybe parade-rainers, but they're not really attracted to us anyway, and of course for $30 they could join and get a T-shirt and other stuff like anyone else."

He laughs and then asks if I know the ethnic make-up of our members? "We don't ask members that," I tell him. "I know we have members ranging in age from eighteen to ninety-one, but I only know that because both those memberships were birthday gifts and the givers told me."

When the Happy Board was up we had born-again Christians, a Wicca warlock, and Buddhists who posted messages, or at least that's what they said they were. "Happiness is the common denominator," I assured him.

After our conversation, I think he understands the concept. He tells me he's a happy person too. I pray this is true, because I need him to sign-off on my prequalification letter.

A week later, the approval comes and I'm a happy camper.

*

Meanwhile, a lot of other things are cooking.

I'm working on the corporate and wellness curriculum. It should be ready by January.

I decide to apply for nonprofit status for the Secret Society of Happy Kids. We can set up a foundation for the children's program and partially fund it with proceeds from product sales. We'll need grants to develop the curriculum for use in schools and youth programs.

I have a new e-mail pal from China. For several weeks, I've received at least one e-mail a week. I can't read the messages because they are in Chinese. I always respond "I can't read Chinese," but they keep sending them. The power of the world wide web amazes me. It's a big Yellow Pages for the world. How did this person find us? I wonder what they want. I have to find someone who reads Chinese.

I also got a sweet note from Alabama Governor Don Siegelman about National Admit You're Happy Day.

November 1999

*I realize that a sense of
humor isn't for everyone.
It's only for people who want to have fun,
enjoy life and feel alive.*

Anne Wilson Schaef

After some bureaucratic delays, my loan is finally approved by The Associates. It won't actually be processed for another month, so it'll be too late for our original plan; create a full line of merchandise for the holiday gift-buying season. But we'll still have some Secret Society of Happy People merchandise for this holiday season.

We sent out a press release with our "Tips for Writing a Holiday Newsletter People Won't Hate to Read" and put samples of funny newsletters on our web site. The Society isn't encouraging or discouraging holiday letter writing. If you don't like reading happy holiday newsletters, just happily throw them in the trash. But since we received so many comments last year, I want to be proactive and share the following tips to help those who want to write a newsletter people will love to read:

Remember who's reading the letter.
Is it family and close friends you keep in touch with on a semi-regular basis or friends you contact only once or twice a year?

The number one complaint about holiday newsletters is that the information doesn't interest the reader. In the convenient era of computers, consider writing two letters: one for family and extremely close friends (the ones you speak to often) and a separate letter for friends you only correspond with during the holidays. Your college pals from twenty years ago probably won't even remember your Aunt Millie, so they really won't be interested that she got a new puppy.

Write like you speak.

You're writing a letter, not a college dissertation. Add funny stories and details to the highlights of your year. You wouldn't call a friend and announce that you just returned from Rome. You'd tell a few of the amusing things that happened on the trip to make it interesting. Your letter should also include the same interesting details.

Be honest.

If your year had a couple of low points, you can mention them without focusing on them. Recounting your year means including the highs and lows. If you've had a particularly depressing year, try to include a few bright spots, even if they seem trivial. You might say, "Even though this year was full of character-building moments (stress, stress, and more stress), I did have some laughs every time I saw a re-run of the *Golden Girls*."

Have a sense of humor.

Hindsight being 20/20, some of the good, bad, and annoying events of the year have probably developed a humorous side in retrospect. Share it because it'll bring a smile to someone's face during a hectic holiday season.

Personalize the letter with a P.S.

It only takes a couple of minutes to make your friend or relative feel special by handwriting a personalized message on the bottom of your newsletter.

We live in a chaotic busy world where we can buy anything except time. Sometimes our annual holiday newsletter is the only way we stay in touch with people who really are important to us. Some of the Society members submitted these newsletters to help you write your own politically correct holiday newsletter and keep your reader laughing.

Letter One: Traditional

Dear Friends,

I always have trouble writing out Christmas cards. I think it's the "annual-ness" of their nature. Despite our uneventful, mundane, basically simple existence, I find it difficult to sum up a year of our lives on a 5 x 7 greeting card. Perhaps the hardest part is remembering everything that's happened in chronological order. As I get a little older, my short-term memory isn't all it used to be. Nonetheless, I am compelled to join the human race in sending out these Season's Greetings!

I finally hung my last panty in July after six years with Victoria's Secret. Though fitting bras and selling intimate apparel to senior citizens can be challenging work, my departure from the mall was tantamount to a religious experience. I've been saved.

I'm working for a small company that's a leading distributor of European equestrian saddles and accessories. We work closely with the riders (and their horses!) to custom fit proper equipment and attire for competitive dressage. The business necessitates traveling to horse shows, most of which are in Florida, from December though April. However, I got home to New Jersey, courtesy of my new job, when we worked a show in Pennsylvania. I enjoy being "on the road," especially when that road leads north. My new job also gives me time to ride my horse every morning. Horsemanship and husbandry are essential in this field, so I'm cramming for the 28 years I've missed.

Kevin is still General Manager of the Sarasota Red Sox and still loves every minute of it. He just got back from the annual Baseball Winter Meetings in Boston—hobnobbing with the big shots. However, he was more excited about his brief encounter with Michael Snipe of R.E.M. in the Atlanta Airport coming home. In the off-season, Kevin coaches two Pee

Wee basketball leagues and manages to hit golf balls on a regular basis. He has also taken up fishing and brain surgery in his spare time.

I hope this holiday season finds you and yours in good spirits (alcohol induced, no doubt). Best wishes for a new year filled with beautiful moments and cherished memories. Please know that we think of you often and smile—remembering only laughter. HAVE A VERY MERRY CHRISTMAS AND HAPPY NEW YEAR!!!!!

Cheers

Chris and Kevin

Letter Two: Multiple Choice

Dear ( )
a)Folks,   b)Auntie and Uncle,   c)Cousin,   d)Friend,

Well here we are at the end of the year,
which for us has been ( )
a) fabulous. b) exciting.
c) interesting. d) lousy.

We're still ( )
a) married b) speaking
c) negotiating d) breathing

and the kids are ( )
a) on the honor roll. b) maintaining a 'C' average.
c) in reform school. d) in foster homes.

For the most part, we're healthy and ( )
a) my skin is finally clearing up.
b) oral surgery isn't so bad if you get the right drugs.
c) I've lost 100 pounds with the help of the electro-shock diet.
d) appreciating Viagra.

Things at work are looking up and I'm ( )
a) being appreciated and recognized for my
   significant contributions.
b) in line for a promotion and my own phone
   extension.
c) still on strike, but bargaining continues.
d) appealing my suspension for downloading pictures
   on the company computer.

We finally took that overseas trip we've been
planning and ( )
a) we only lost two bags.
b) we got sick on the bottled water!
c) they really don't like Americans, do they?
d) Dorothy was right.

At least we learned ( )
a) it's easier to pay the ransom.
b) never joke with a customs official wearing
   rubber gloves.
c) bring your own toilet paper.
d) if you can't speak the language, don't use sign
   language to order in a restaurant.

We're now looking ahead to the New Year and wish
you and yours ( )
a) the happiest of holidays.
b) a festive and prosperous New Year.
c) better luck than we've had.
d) a successful bond reduction hearing.

Happy Holidays!

The Smiths

Letter Three: Braggers' Favorite

Dear family and friends,

It's so difficult to sum up my exciting and glorious year, but here are my Top Ten Highlights:

10. I'm finally driving my dream car—one without payments.

9. Took an international vacation—I crossed the border when I was in California. We can't remember the name of the town, but the tequila was worth the trip.

8. Finally lost that 10 pounds I promised I would lose (who's counting the five I gained).

7. Had a garage sale to sell all of my old bridesmaid dresses—made $100 and cleaned out a big corner in my closet to put the new clothes that I don't wear.

6. Took up golf—I own clubs, shoes, and an outfit, so I look great but my swing isn't worth mentioning.

5. Visited my parents (trying to stay in the will) and Mom insisted on taking me shopping. I couldn't disappoint her.

4. Thanks to all of my out-of-town friends and family I accumulated a free airline ticket from the miles I'm awarded for every dollar I spend on long-distance.

3. I babysat my neighbor's dog and decided that I'm not ready to be a dog mommy—too much responsibility at my age (I'm not telling).

2. Went snow skiing, looked great in my new outfit not mentioning the tree or my new nose.

1. Kissed so many frogs (lots of blind dates) this year that I'm expecting to meet my prince next year (I'm told it's a numbers game so it's got to be my turn). I'm warning you now to start saving for my engagement present.

Hoping you and your loved ones had an equally exciting and wonderful year with an even better one coming up.

Happy Holiday's,

Susan

Letter Four: Traditional

Dear Friends,

Well, December finds us on the move again. Mobile, Alabama, this time. Located in southwest Alabama, Mobile is 31 miles north of the Gulf of Mexico, 141 miles east of New Orleans, and only 56 miles from Florida's beaches (a vain attempt to encourage visitors). Kevin has accepted a position with the Mobile Baybears—AA affiliate of the San Diego Padres. Another step up the ladder of success! We are currently in the midst of looking for a home (always a challenge with two dogs and a horse) and a new job for me (my favorite past-time—NOT!). We should be completely moved in by the end of January and will forward our new address and phone to the select few we don't owe money to at the moment.

I'm still horsin' around, recreationally and "professionally"—I use this word loosely. I just keep working in the international equestrian field. Donned in jean shorts and a tee-shirt, I mosey into the office at 10 P.M. and spend the next eight hours trading horse stories with people from all over the world. Not a high stress environment.

Happily, we were able to visit with some of our good friends across the miles this past year— fondly remembering Jill's wedding and Thanksgiving in Myrtle! Here's to friendships of a lifetime... YADDA...YADDA...YADDA...!

These sappy Christmas letters are all the same, aren't they? An annual synopsis of achievements, promotions, exotic vacations, major purchases, new additions to the family, and general good times. An obvious embellishment of our rather mundane lives. An unsolicited bragging session filled with glad tidings and inspirational prose. It is with some trepidation and a twisted sense of humor that I share our reality with you.

I turned 30 last month—yikes! Kevin is experiencing a major golf slump, money is tight, and we're ready to strangle the next idiot who asks when we're going to have children.

Hoping this holiday season finds you all in good health and spirits!

With all our love,

Kevin and Chris

Letter Five: Fill-in-the-Blank

Dear _____ (Relative you haven't heard from since last Christmas),

We hope this Holiday Season finds you and _____ (pet name) happy and well. Things at our homestead have been _____ (happy adjective) but the weather is absolutely _____ (synonym for awful).

You may remember that last year I worked for the local _____ (type of fertilizer) plant. Well, things finally went my way and now I head the entire _____ (color) department! You can bet that we've had a hand in every new advancement for better _____ (household appliance, plural).

Because of my promotion, we got rid of our 12-year-old _____ (inexpensive foreign car) and are now driving a swanky new _____ (breed of dog). As for the rest of the family, _____ (old fashioned woman's name) is fine and now chairs the local Society for the Preservation of _____ (type of fruit). Because of her busy schedule she has little time for the volunteer work she used to do at the _____ (type of municipal building), but still enjoys _____ (word ending in -ing) around in her beloved garden.

Eldest daughter _____ (trendy girl's name) still attends the prestigious _____ (royal family name) Academy and continues to make high marks in _____ (Oriental country, as an adjective) literature. She also plays _____ (profession) for the school's _____ (vegetable) squad, which this year won the coveted _____ (radioactive element) Cup.

Our son, _____ (carrion-eating bird), Junior, is finally through with his exams and looks forward to his final semester of _____ (type of crime). He should graduate in June and looks forward to attending _____ (brand of cigar) College this fall.

All of us are in good health, other than the usual recurring problems with my _____ (body part), which hasn't been quite right since that accident when we were kids. It still makes me _____(bodily function) to think about it!

    Well, that about wraps things up from
_____ (city in North Dakota). As we
expressed in our card, have a _____(word
ending in -ly) Christmas and a prosperous
_____ (year during the Civil War).

    Much love to the entire _____ (zoo
animal) family,

Your Cousin,
_____ (one of the 7 Dwarfs).

I hope people will appreciate the humorous message in these.
Holiday newsletters just need to be fun. You can say almost anything
as long as it's funny. I wonder what Ann will say about holiday
newsletters this year? Can't believe it's already been a whole year.

At the end of the month I close my SBA secured loan. I'm very
happy thanks to The Associates, Shirley for believing in the Society
enough to process my loan, Ron from the SBA office, and Jim from
the SBDC. Yes, the Society will finally be able to become a business
with the mission of encouraging the expression of happiness.

December 1999

We never did get a public apology from Ann Landers for holiday newsletter writers. People are calling me now to tell me she ran that column again, telling people not to send happy holiday newsletters. It still amazes me that so much fuss is created by a piece of paper about the happy things that happened to someone in the course of a year.

We sent out our press release about the Happiest Events and Moments of 1999 earlier in December than we did last year. I hope nothing "too happy" happens during the rest of the month.

The Happiest Events and Moments for 1999 are

10. La Vida Loca has people swinging their hips for the first time since Elvis.
9. Susan Lucci finally wins a daytime Emmy.
8. The U.S. women's soccer team wins the World Cup.
7. Lance Armstrong wins the Tour de France.
6. *Who Wants to Be a Millionaire* makes ABC and America very happy.

5. For conservative, compassionate Republicans, Pat Buchanan departs from the party.
4. Kosovo families are reunited.
3. We're finally done with Monica and Ken Starr.
2. Roberto Benigni becomes the happiest person alive during his *Life Is Beautiful* Oscar acceptance speeches.
1. No more pre-Y2K hype.

The Society is now on several members' holiday newsletter lists. It's fun getting cards from people I really don't know. Maybe one day we'll have a "Happy Museum" for all of the stuff we've been sent. One card stands out. The card from Alabama's Governor Don Siegelman includes an invitation to the Holiday Tree Lighting Party at the governor's mansion. Alabama must have the happiest governor.

I decide to postpone giving the "Not Letting Anyone Rain on Their Parade" awards until August, so we have something special for Admit You're Happy Month. The celebration of Admit You're Happy Day will now be a month because that gives members and chapters more time to do something in their cities. It'll be nice to give out awards then.

Got an e-mail from CNN. Jeanne Moos wants to include our Happiest Events, Inventions, and Social Changes of the Century in a story about millennium lists.

We do a phone interview. Her video will show the picture of me at an outhouse since indoor plumbing received the most votes for the happiest invention of the century.

During the interview, Jeanne says, "We could have done a whole story about your list." All I could think was, "that's why I sent you the press release" but there's always next time.

CNN runs the Jeanne Moos list story a number of times during the days before the new year. It's great because it includes our logo, our list, and a picture of me in an outhouse!

On the Sunday after Christmas, my friend Mark calls and leaves me a message, "Congratulations you made it in to *Parade* magazine." We've been sending them press releases, but they hadn't interviewed me, so I am very curious to see what they wrote.

I immediately find the *Parade* insert. The cover announces "The Best and Worst of Everything." As I flip through the pages, I see in big red letters "Best List of the Century." Voila! Here's our story about the 100 Happiest Events, Inventions and Social Changes list, which *Parade* found in the *San Francisco Chronicle*.

What a great Christmas present!

Despite this happy news I had a pang of frustration because a list that *Parade* magazine called the "Best List of the Century" wasn't even covered by the Associated Press. They're still worried about giving "happiness" or "the Society" too much coverage. We'd only be so lucky if they reviewed the coverage they give scandals, crime, and gossip with the same rigid standards.

Despite this moment of frustration, I realize it's only a fleeting moment. Overall I'm ecstatic that since the Society began receiving media attention we'd made great headway into getting people to talk about the expression of happiness. Our message was becoming part of the American culture, and we were positively impacting others.

I wonder what adventures 2000 will bring for the Society and if I'm ready for them?

January 2000

The most revolutionary thing we can do in this culture is be happy.

Dr. Patch Adams

This month I've been busy writing my book and preparing for the Dallas Market Center Gift Show, it's where buyers from small to large stores pick out the merchandise they sell. Since our stuff is so unique, funny, and inspirational, I decided to introduce our merchandise line at the show.

The night before the show, one of my friends who's going to help me at the booth receives the news that her brother, who was only forty-seven years old, a husband, and the father of three girls, had been killed in a car accident that afternoon. She comes from a family of ten children, and I'm close to three of the sisters.

Needless to say, when you're close to three people who are dealing with an enormous amount of shock and grief, it has an effect on you. It's not as if the death were in my own backyard, but it's definitely in my playground.

The pain my friends are going through is almost unbearable to watch because there really isn't anything that I can do to help take it away. I can be there, listen, laugh and cry with them, but it's not like I can put a Band-Aid on the boo-boo and make it better. It's one of those experiences that only time will heal.

Of course being so close to this unhappy moment that's causing so much pain for people I love has me contemplating the message of the Society. I wonder if we're frivolous and unnecessary.

But as I'm talking to one of the sisters it occurs to me that the opposite is true. The reason the message of the Society is so important is that life can be too short and people experience pain. But you also experience happiness and you need to cherish it.

If as a culture we can't start embracing and sharing our happy moments, we'll surely become a society where remembering our illnesses, tragedies, and depressing moments are the norm and not the exception to our personal scrapbook we call our life. When someone reads our eulogy, will we want them to speak of the moments that defined our pain, or will we want them to recall the moments of happiness that we experienced and brought to others?

If we don't express these moments how can we expect others to do it.

I'm again reminded through an experience that I wouldn't have thought would bring me a lesson about happiness; that we should indeed live life to its fullest and that includes being happy, encouraging others to be happy, and talking about happiness.

February 2000

Happiness is knowing a flower
will grow where you've planted a seed.

Anonymous

I spoke with a producer from a national television show, and she asked me, "Why did you start the Society?" I immediately responded by explaining the "cultural needs" for the Society and my funny daydream of a group of people just talking about "happy stuff." Again she asked, "What do you personally get out of it?" I think I gave her a quick answer that didn't really do justice to what I get out of it, but I pondered the question for the next couple of days.

I believe that somewhere between the *Ed Sullivan* and the *Jerry Springer* era we quit talking about happiness. It's not that we quit being happy but we forgot that expressing it is important. It's part of being a balanced person. Rarely is happiness inclusive or exclusive to any experience but neither is misery. As we quit expressing happiness we also became more inclined to rain on people's parades (including our own). The Society is just a way for me to encourage people to think about happiness in a different light.

When I refer to the Society I usually do it in terms of "we." People often ask who the "we" is and as far as the details (fielding phone calls, organizing the web site, buying the merchandise, writing the newsletter, sending press releases, mailing everything, and on and on) to make the Society a reality, it's 90 percent me. But the "we" I refer to are the millions of people who understand and believe in the message of the Society. I've just been blessed to be the voice that's put it all together.

✳

I sent President Clinton a request for a national proclamation declaring August Admit You're Happy Month. Next year we'll try to get a proclamation from the United Nations, afterall we are an international organization and happiness is a universal experience. I wonder if President Clinton will give us a proclamation.

✳

My mother calls me and tells me to read the Ann Landers column (February 20). I immediately find it and the headline reads, "Christmas newsletters win reader's approval." This of course happily caught my attention. Ann says, "It's nearly March, and I am still getting letters clobbering me for my column knocking Christmas newsletters. The verdict is clear 100 – 1. I lose." (She ran the same "don't write holiday newsletter" column in December 1999 that she did in November 1998).

This is followed by several letters from people who like reading holiday newsletters or at least believe that people have the right to write them. My personal favorite is from someone in Sioux City, Iowa: "If you don't like Christmas letters, don't read them. But be aware that a lot of people appreciate them, so please don't rain on our parade."

I wonder if that writer has read about the Secret Society of Happy People. Obviously, he or she is a member in spirit.

Even though the Society wasn't mentioned in Ann's column, I wonder if it was our response in 1998 that inspired her readers to write to her this year when they read her column discouraging people from sending holiday newsletters.

It really doesn't matter. I'm just delighted that Ann finally agrees that people have the *right* to share happy holiday news.

Welcome to the Secret Society of Happy People!

*The surest way to happiness is in losing yourself
in a cause greater than yourself.*

Anonymous

Part Two

How Many Types
of Happiness Are There?

Let Me Count the Smiles

Happiness is a butterfly,
which, when pursued,
is always just beyond your grasp,
but which if you will sit down quietly,
may alight upon you.

Nathaniel Hawthorne

Are You Happier Than You Admit You Are? is the slogan for the Society membership T-shirt and bumper sticker because it reflects the first question we want to encourage people to think about. Are they happier than what they are talking about?

Of course, when you start asking the tough questions, it's only natural that people start asking you for the answers. The Society didn't want to get into the business of telling people to be happy or how to be happy or even define what happiness is.

Happiness is an experience that's different for everyone. The Society just wants people to recognize happy experiences when they are happening and give them the attention they deserve.

One thing I recognized was that people tended to put happiness into the categories of humor, fun, and gratitude. So I asked myself, "How many types of happiness are there?"

I thought that if we could help people broaden their definition of happy experiences then it would help them recognize happiness and thus talk about it more.

So I began the quest to find the Types of Happiness. With little effort I initially came up with eighteen Types of Happiness. Once that was published in our newsletter and listed on the web site, people suggested more types and we've increased the number to twenty-one Types of Happiness:

Amusement
A feeling of entertainment and delight.

Anticipation
When we're on the verge of experiencing
something we've hoped for,
or we're daydreaming about the possibilities
of our hopes, dreams, and wishes.

Bittersweet
A feeling of fond nostalgia with an overlay of sadness.

Borrowed
When we allow ourselves to share in another person's happy moment.

Celebration
Part of the rituals associated with holidays, births,
weddings, graduations, anniversaries, and achievements.

Cheerful
The gladness that enables people to express themselves
in a way that brings joy and excitement to others.

Contentment
When we're happy with our current situation.

Exuberance
A full-of-life feeling that creates a positive energy
that exudes from our soul.

Fun
Gained through playful experiences.

Giving
The custom of giving gifts, time, and love
can bring the expression of happiness to life
for the giver and recipient.

Grateful
Recognizing and appreciating gifts, lessons, and opportunities.

Humor
Our ability to laugh at everything,
including the good, bad, and sometimes ugly.

Joyful
The feeling of delight from an experience
that's expressed with a visible radiance.

Love
The warmth of tender or passionate affection.

Peaceful
A feeling of tranquillity, calm, and quiet.

Playful
Engaging in activities that are amusing, fun, or recreational.

Relief
Lightening of a burden and the ease of anxiety.

Satisfaction
The gratification you feel after you've fulfilled
a need, wish, or expectation.

Spiritual
The feeling one gets when the soul is connected to a divine order.

Surprise
Finding delight in the unexpected.

Sweet
The small kindnesses that people witness and experience
that are often unexpected.

Of course, you're welcome to submit any type you think we may have forgotten.

This section will feature stories, essays, vignettes, poems, and songs that will highlight each type of happiness. Without a doubt you'll recognize that these stories aren't inclusive to the type of happiness they represent, but I did try to put them in the categories that they best depicted. They may very easily represent another category for you because the experience of happiness is subjective to the person who's experiencing it.

Whether the pieces are funny, ironic, subtle, or poignant, I hope that all of them will delight you.

*We miss the really great joys of life
scrambling for bargain-counter happiness.*

Roy L. Smith

Amusement

A smile is a curve that sets everything straight.

Anonymous

Your Kids Are Listening

Cindy incorporates the philosophy of the Society into her daily life. That includes recognizing "happy moments" and discussing the different types of happiness with her kids.

One day she and her daughter Jamie, a senior in high school, were out running errands. Jamie enthusiastically told her mother that since she was working more hours at her part-time job, she wanted to buy a newer car. When she turned sixteen, Jamie, like many kids, inherited an older car. Jamie explained in great detail about how she could afford a newer car. This way she'd have it when she went away to college next year.

Of course, Cindy went into her role of mother and protector. She started asking, "Have you thought about insurance?" and "What if you start working fewer hours when you start college?"

Jamie turned, smiled, and softly said, "Mom, don't even think of raining on my parade."

At this moment Cindy stopped and laughed because she hadn't meant to be a parade-rainer. She realized that this was an opportunity for her to *walk her talk* and be excited with Jamie about her goal. And it was even nicer to know that her daughter listened.

As told to PJ

The Wish List

Remember the old adage, "Be careful what you wish for, you just might get it?" Well, Richard learned that sometimes you almost get things that you wished for only as a joke.

In his new job as a manager, Richard prepared to submit his first departmental budget. His boss told him, "Always include absolutely everything you could possibly want in your budget 'wish list,' because lots of the things on the list won't be approved."

Richard understood that the initial budget list was just part of the dance between the various levels of management. One level would ask for something (even if they didn't really want it) so another level could say, "no." Richard knew, if this traditional corporate dance didn't happen, the bean counters would think they weren't doing their jobs.

For kicks, Richard decided he would ask for a hot tub for his office. That would give them something to cut. He put it in his budget request. After all, his boss had said, "Your budget is your wish list."

Richard thought that his boss would see it, laugh, and cut it. But to Richard's great surprise, his hot tub request sailed through. It passed his boss and three more levels of management. It only had to clear one more level before Richard would find himself picking out a new hot tub for his office. He was shocked, but he was also beginning to get a little excited about this possibility. Green marble would be nice, he thought, or maybe a granite look.

Alas, at the last check-point, Richard's request for a hot tub was finally denied. Nonetheless, he was pretty amused.

Even if the big bosses weren't.

As told to PJ

114

Anticipation

The soul should always stand ajar,
ready to welcome the ecstatic experience.

Emily Dickinson

Daydreams about Cancun

Debby's husband, Glenn, called her at work and enthusiastically announced, "The local radio station just called my name to win $100 per hour, until the next person hears their name called and calls in, and I'll also be in a drawing for a trip for two to Cancun, Mexico."

It was in the middle of a Minnesota winter and a trip to sunny, warm Cancun sounded even more appealing than usual. Debby was so excited about the possibility of winning the trip that she really didn't even pay attention to the $100 per hour her husband had just won.

She spent the afternoon looking at the snow outside her office window and daydreaming about being on the beach.

Debby was certain her husband was meant to win this trip and that she'd be heading to the beach for a week of R and R, so she started looking at catalogs to see what new clothes she would buy for her beach vacation.

In the meantime, Glenn called all his friends to tell them he was in the running for a vacation and to listen for his name to be drawn at 5:00 P.M. He eagerly listened to see how many $100 hours would go by, until someone else called. But after only one hour, the next person whose name was announced called the station.

Although Glenn won only $100, he still had high hopes of hearing his name drawn at 5:00 P.M. and taking off for Cancun.

When Debby and Glenn got home from work, they continued to fantasize about a week in Cancun. Finally, at five o'clock the announcement came. But it wasn't Glenn's name. Debby, so certain they'd be off to Cancun, was shocked. Glenn was still excited that he'd won that $100.

"Just anticipating that we might win was one of the best after-noons I'd had in a long time," Debby says wistfully. "I just knew Glenn was going to win. Oh, well, this way I didn't actually have to try on swimsuits, I just got to have fun thinking about it."

As told to PJ

Bittersweet

Even a happy life cannot be without a measure of darkness,
and the word "happiness" would lose its meaning
if it were not balanced by sadness.

Carl Jung

Dental Karma

It began with a chipped tooth. For the past five years I had successfully avoided going to the dentist by endlessly brushing and flossing. And then one day, I had no choice but to go. A sip of cold Coca-Cola crept into my tooth, reached the nerve, and excruciating pain shot through my jaw.

My fear of the dentist is like most people's fear of death. Just the aroma of a dentist's office is enough to induce a panic attack: My blood pressure skyrockets, and that's quickly followed by nausea and cold sweats.

A friend recommended "the best dentist in town," adding, "Oh, by the way, he's cute, single and available." Given my pain, cute and single weren't important criteria in a dentist, although I admitted it would give me a chance to see her definition of cute. It had been a few months since I had broken up with the love of my life and men were finally moving beyond the category of "scum of the earth."

From the chair in the examining room I could hear him talking to the other victims. I hadn't seen him yet, but I could tell he would've made a great Billy Crystal. I was interested.

My heart skipped a beat when I finally saw him, and not because of dental phobia, but because I wanted to toss the hygienist out the door, pull him into my chair, and rip his clothes off. At that moment, I understood the hormonal urges of teenage boys.

What a dentist! Your basic tall, dark, and handsome—six feet, four inches, athletic, lean, and hypnotic hazel eyes that made me melt. As he was checking me for TMJ, quivers ran through my body when he touched my neck and shoulders. I wanted more.

"Your tooth is chipped," he confirmed. I would have to return, and for the first time in my life, I was grateful that a dentist had requested my presence. Even better, he was suggesting more chair time. "Your wisdom teeth are impacted," he said. "They have to be removed."

Usually, I would have been horrified at the thought, but now I simply wondered if it would be appropriate if I showed up for my next appointment wearing a little silk number from Victoria's Secret.

The karma had begun.

I waited for the appointment with mixed emotions: fear of the dental procedure, and lust for the dentist. The lust won out and I arrived in a new dress.

"A dental tech is with us at all times," he joked, "but if the laughing gas makes you get a little wild and you want to get rid of her let me know."

Could he read my mind? Would laughing gas induce true confessions? He told me I had beautiful eyes. Was he sincere? I was hooked. I started praying I would see him somewhere other than his office.

My next appointment fell months later. By then, my lust had waned, though it certainly wasn't forgotten. When the hygienist finished my routine cleaning, the dentist spoke up from the next room, saying that he'd be right in to check my teeth.

The hygienist answered, "It's not necessary. She's fine." I wanted to slap her.

"Doesn't Pam want to see me?" he asked. I wanted to yell, "Yes, and preferably naked," but my mouth was full.

As I left, he waved, "Did you lose weight?" he asked. I wanted to marry this guy.

The next time I saw him was to have my wisdom teeth out. By the time the day of my appointment arrived, my fear outweighed my lust. I dressed for in-office surgery: sweats, no make-up. He explained all the possible complications, but I was confident there wouldn't be any, even though I secretly relished the idea of returning again and again. Then he asked for two copies of the dreamy Pachelbel's Canon tape I had in my Walkman to listen to during the procedure—one for him and one for his assistant. Why would he buy her a tape? I wondered. Then I remembered: He was a prince charming, so he was probably just being nice.

The wheels of karma continued. The following week, when I returned to have my stitches removed, I got bad news for my mouth but good news for my strong desire to keep seeing my dentist. "The incisions in your lower jaws aren't healing well," he said. "We'll need to pack them."

For the next month I was in his office once a week. His flirtations continued. He was the first man I'd been attracted to in months and he appeared interested, but he never asked me out. I was getting frustrated. What was my dental karma?

Finally, the last of the packing was removed and I only had one appointment left, a dental cleaning. I was relieved, actually. I needed to quit seeing this man if nothing was going to happen between us.

"Now you have a chipped filling," the hygienist said during my cleaning. "It'll need to be repaired right away." Instead of being happy to come back and see my dream dentist, yet again, I left feeling vaguely angry, frustrated, and annoyed. If he was only going to flirt, but not ask me out, then I wanted this dental karma to stop!

Fortunately, or unfortunately, the universe heard my pleas.

A week later, while in the waiting room I was working on an article about intimacy. His assistant (the same one he bought the tape for) called me in, and I continued writing my article while in the dental chair waiting for him.

"What are you working on?" the assistant asked. I told her and she asked to read it. She even urged me to read it to my dentist. I thought this was strange, but why not? When he came into the room, she mentioned the topic, he laughed and made a joke about sex.

"Intimacy and sex are not the same thing," I remarked.

After my tooth was filled and he left the room, his assistant, a beautiful brunette with dazzling eyes, confided quietly, "He has a problem with intimacy. We've been seeing each other a lot. He should read your article."

My heart sank. How could he flirt with me while he was dating her?

The next day, I mailed both of them copies of an intimacy worksheet I had among my research material, along with my business card, still hoping he would call.

But as suddenly as it had appeared, my dental karma slipped

away. The only dental problem I had now was my bill.

A few weeks later, the phone rang at my desk.

"I have good news and bad news," a friend who'd just returned from an appointment with my dentist said. "The good news is I know what your dental karma was. The bad news is the dentist is now engaged to his assistant."

"How can that be?" I gasped. "Two weeks ago, he could barely commit to dating her!"

"Maybe it was the intimacy information you mailed them," she suggested.

Karma sucks.

Maybe if it weren't for me they wouldn't be planning a life of wedded bliss. It's not that I wasn't happy to be of service, but instead of being the fairy godmother, I'd rather have been his Cinderella.

PJ

Borrowed

To be able to share in another's joy,
that is the secret of happiness.

George Bernanos

Daughter of the Bride

Starting a story with a cliché isn't too original but sometimes the shoe fits and you should wear it.

Mothers and daughters begin planning "The Wedding" from the time of birth. The daughter's birth, that is. I always thought the focus of the dream was the daughter's wedding, not the mother's.

I was wrong. It started with a phone call. My long-divorced mother was engaged. She shared in great detail the story of the proposal, the ring, and finally the fact she was going to have the wedding at a church. It's the same conversation that you've had a million times with sisters, girlfriends, and women you meet in passing, but the last person I ever thought I'd have it with was my mother. Not that I didn't expect her to remarry, but I didn't expect to plan her wedding before we planned mine.

The next evening, my aunt phoned. She was anxious to begin the wedding planning. I was still recovering from my disappointment that it wasn't my wedding we were planning. To make matters worse, I was approaching the big 3-0 and there wasn't even a man in my life who I'd want to marry.

I received my assignments and a date was picked to go shopping for the wedding dress. I wasn't sure if I should buy the usual gift I give my friends who are planning a wedding: the latest copy of *Bride* magazine.

What was the appropriate engagement gift for your own mother? Was I supposed to host a bridal shower?

I researched the proper etiquette for the daughter of the bride. I didn't find anything written about the do's and don'ts. I was beginning to feel that I was the only daughter in the world who was confused by playing this particular role.

My mother, aunt, and a cousin I didn't know very well showed up at my door on the designated day to go shopping for the wedding attire. Listening to the three of them talk about the men in their lives, the gifts of jewelry received from these men and sex was enough to make me want to skip the shopping trip. But as the dutiful daughter of the bride I suggested we get started. I had decided that I would buy the dress as my engagement gift. A bride shouldn't buy her own dress, even if she is your mother.

Plans filled the six weeks before the wedding. During every conversation with my mother, she went over what had been done and what needed to be done in great detail. She kept giving me additional assignments, including buying the gown for her wedding night. I didn't even want to think about my mom on a romantic honeymoon.

I recognized that she was nervous and excited about the big day that would begin the rest of her life with her new husband, but I was getting tired of the check list and wanted to scream. Are all brides this way? Will I be this annoying to her when I'm planning my own wedding? I hope so.

The next challenge was the wedding gift. What does one give their mom? She didn't register a gift list. I didn't know her fiancé's taste in anything. After many hours of searching malls and gift shops, I finally settled on flatware.

My brother and I arrived at Mom's house on the big day. My mother informed my brother that he would be a bridesperson instead of giving her away as originally planned. He took it with good humor. We walked down the aisle followed by the bride. The bride and groom said their vows, kissed, and the ceremony was over. I arrived that day with one small family. With an exchange of "I do's" and a kiss, my family had instantly grown to too many people to count. My holidays would never be the same.

The photographs of the new family were taken and the reception began. People who I don't remember ever meeting were talking to me as though I'd known them all my life. I pretended I knew them; it was just easier that way.

The bride threw the bouquet and, fortunately, my cousin's three-year-old daughter caught it. Anytime the merrymakers at a wedding gather up all the unmarried women so the bouquet can be thrown, I want to tell everyone I'm really married. He works for the CIA. He is overseas on assignment. They don't know him because his job is top secret. It would be too dangerous if even his own in-laws could recognize him. Wishful thinking.

The groom threw the garter, and then Mom and her new husband were off to honeymoon.

I thought about the ceremony and what the day had really meant. It went far beyond unknown relations and uncaught bouquets. I had watched my mother change from a woman who thought she'd never love again to a blushing bride full of the hope and joy that falling in love brings.

And at that moment, I was happy to be the daughter of the bride.

PJ

Celebration

I once wanted to become an atheist, but I gave up—
they have no holidays.

Henny Youngman

You're Invited to a Party...Bring Soap

When I heard the knock at my door, I didn't want to answer it
because I knew who it was—the delivery guy. His arrival
meant that I had crossed the threshold into full-fledged adulthood: I'd
bought a washer and dryer.

I felt depressed about the financial investment required to own
equipment that cleans clothing. I think those appliances should be
included in my apartment, just like my refrigerator, stove, and dish-
washer. In fact, in my last apartment I refused to cross this particular
adulthood threshold. Instead, I just rented a washer and dryer. When I
added up the monthly payments, however, it became obvious that I
could've bought the pair, plus a couple of tons of detergent for what
I'd paid in rent alone. This is not to say that I mind being an adult, but
as a younger adult, I would've taken the washer-dryer acquisition
money and gone skiing.

At that time in my life, I would have ignored the slight inconven-
ience of walking to the apartment complex's communal laundry room.
As a full-fledged adult, however, the idea of carrying laundry to the
laundry room in all kinds weather, only to wait in line for bad equipment, is unthinkable. Now, I'd rather spend my money on home con-
veniences than go on a vacation. Yes, I've crossed the grownup
threshold.

As a young adult, I saw major purchases such as my first sofa or a
new car as rites of passage. My friends and family got excited. I held
a housewarming party to welcome my new furniture. I took my
friends for rides in my new car—well, it was new to me.

But, no one ever says, "I just got a brand new washer and dryer.

Let's have a laundry party at my house!" A child never thinks, "I can't wait until I'm old enough to buy my very own washer and dryer!"

For now, my credit card bill is a monthly reminder that I didn't escape the inevitable: full-fledged adulthood complete with washer-dryer payments. I'm trying to cope by doing lots of laundry. I have decided to cross this threshold with dignity. I'll begin by turning my wistful tears over the loss of youth into celebrations, laughter, and hope for the promise my salesman made: I won't need to buy another washer and dryer for twenty years.

PJ

What's Valentine's Day Meant to be Anyway?

The day unattached singles dread, February 14, rolled around. Julie wasn't dating anyone seriously, one of her friends had just broken up with her fiancé, another friend wasn't dating, and another friend's husband had to work that night. Instead of being alone or blue, the four women decided to make it a girls' night out.

They bought a couple of bottles of wine, a bottle of champagne, and fifty chocolate-covered strawberries. Unbeknownst to each other, they each brought flowers. They spent the evening with all the usual Valentine's Day trappings.

They watched movies, laughed, and danced. Finally around midnight, they fell asleep on the couches.

When Julie woke up, she realized this had been one of the best Valentine evenings she'd ever had. It was a completely stressless evening, full of merry-making and unburdened by expectations or pressure.

Julie had to stop and think about how we're so wrapped up in the supposed romance of Valentine's Day, we forget to celebrate other important loving relationships that are significant to us. After all, Cupid's arrows are really about love, not just romance.

As told to PJ

Cheerful

Nap Time Blues

A three-year-old sings to a blues beat...

[CHORUS]

I got the nap time blues—
    I don't want to go to bed.
I got the nap time blues—
    I am not a sleepy head.
I refuse to snooze,
    I don't care what Mommy said!

I woke up this morning,
    I was glad to be alive—
Big hand on the twelve,
    Small hand on the five.

Sucked my thumb a little,
    Crawled out of my crib.
Fixed my favorite breakfast (chocolate cake!)
    And I did not use a bib!

[REPEAT CHORUS]

I spent the morning playing
    With my favorite set of toys
They make the biggest messes!
    They make the loudest noise!

When lunch-time rolled around,
    I ate my carrots strained.
Some day I'll eat 'em crunchy,
    Some day I'll be potty-trained!

[REPEAT CHORUS]

I'm a kid of action,
    I'm always on the go—
When it comes to nap time,
    I hate to stop the show…!

For about a half-a-minute,
    We played in the park.
Then Mom said, "Time for beddy-bye,"
    I said, "It isn't even dark!"

[REPEAT CHORUS]

By David C. Perry

The Project

Each week the Women's Medicine Circle that I'm a member of passes around the talking stick. It's the time when each person checks in with all of their news: the good, bad, and mundane.

On this particular evening the last person to receive the talking stick after listening to eight others' "stuff" is Betty. She immediately looks down at the talking stick and pops out a giggle that reminds me of the Pillsbury Doughboy's giggle. Everyone can't help but smile because of her infectious laugh. She says, "It's been an interesting week."

Betty takes a deep breath and says she's been very busy at work, where she's a nurse at the jail. She also states she's been juggling several doctor appointments. Then mentions a few more personal encounters and says, "but I think I'm doing really good."

Next she announces, "My biggest challenge and fear is that my uterine biopsy came back positive for cancer."

The group is somber; we wait to hear her express how she feels. We want to support her. We're so focused we can feel her breathing rhythm and the fear hiding deep within her. Then she laughs and chuckles.

Betty says, "I think its really kinda funny, you know? I mean, it's ironic. I specialized in oncology nursing and here I go and get cancer!" And she giggles and chuckles some more. "They wanna do some more tests and there's this new drug out that's supposed to be really good with this kind of cancer." And she talks some more in a matter-of-fact way about the details and doctors while she looks at each of us around the Circle, straight in the eye, and beams and smiles when she connects with each of us as she talks. I think she could feel the love coming from each of us.

Then our Circle facilitator offers our services to her. We all nod and interject our various talents, disciplines, focuses, and training.

A little teary-eyed, Betty says, "Thank you all. I appreciate your help." And she quickly goes back to expressing some more about the irony of this illness in her life. She is still giggling and laughing and shaking her head.

Then the Circle facilitator asks her if she has thought about this illness in her Warrior work this season, which is the North, the

Walk-Your-Talk area of the Medicine Circle, and she stuns us AGAIN!

"I think I created this illness because I didn't have anything to do. I mean, it is my field, and I'm really not working in it anymore at the jail...." She pauses and says, "...and I think I'm going to beat it. I just needed 'a project,'—that's all. I was bored." And she titters.

We can't help but laugh too. Have you ever in your wildest moments heard someone refer to his or her life-threatening illness as a project that person created because he or she is bored? And in the next breath laugh and indicate he or she will remedy the situation? Betty has the most amazing, upbeat, and infectious good spirit.

If there's any truth that a person's attitude helps them heal, then Betty already is on the road to recovery. Her cheerful attitude and innate happy spirit will work a miracle to heal her.

By T. Dominy

Contentment

Success is getting and achieving what you want.
Happiness is wanting and being content with what you get.

Bernard Meltzer

Guy Heaven

Brian and Melissa lived in Kansas City and had been dating seriously for several months when Brian was offered a job in St. Louis in the marketing department of a large national brewery. Brian had to move to St. Louis right away and he asked Melissa to join him as soon as she could. Melissa arrived in St. Louis a few weeks later, and began her job search.

One day, Brian came home from work and found his apartment full of satellite dish equipment. What was going on? Melissa had just gotten a job selling satellite dish equipment and services.

"I was suddenly living every man's dream," Brian jokes gratefully. "I was in Guy Heaven. I had my favorite girl, every channel in the world, and all the beer I could ever want."

As told to PJ

The Best Job

Iknow what my job is; I am my kids' chauffeur. Or, as Dr. Laura would say, "I am my kids' Mom." It seems to amount to just about the same thing.

I like my job, except for cleaning up the house, but now and then I do think about other things I might do. For instance, I found an article in a magazine called *POV* (November 1998) written by man named Mark Lotto (does he win, I wonder?) about another man named Ron Douglas who, at age 33, has the best job ever.

He is a "flavor developer" for Ben and Jerry's Ice Cream. So where do I go to sign up for that gig?

Douglas describes one facet of his job like this: "We do mega-dessert eating. We go out to eat, order all of the desserts on the menu, then sit around the table and play 'pass the plate.' You eat dessert, eat dessert, eat dessert. Then we come back to the lab, check our supplies, order any ingredients we need, and try to concoct ice cream flavors that reflect the more popular desserts we're seeing around the country."

As my sainted grandmother would have said, "From this he makes a living?"

Because I've piqued your curiosity, I'll note that Douglas also says that his personal favorite flavor is Vanilla Caramel Fudge Swirl, that the downside to the job is the calories involved, and that his roommate is a dentist so, "I can eat all the ice cream and he fixes my teeth."

This beats working, as far as I can tell, and if it involved just a little writing, it would strike me as about the best job on the planet.

I can think of a few other jobs that might compare.

I wouldn't mind a food-testing or creating job, in that I know just how to eat. However, I have some additional areas of expertise to offer the job market.

It would be fun, for instance, to be a buyer for the library, which would tap into one of my big skills: the ability to spend money on books. Along those lines, I could sign up to be a book reviewer (something I've actually done once or twice) or a "reader" who screens manuscripts for a publisher. I could happily read all day if an occasional cup of coffee came my way.

Maybe I could test things. I could test mattresses (just watch me nap—now there's something I do really well). I would be simply wonderful at testing bubble bath. I would happily test sleek cars. Imagine tooling around in some expensive sports car (top down, of course) just to find out if it can stand up to the rigors of a carpool. Within the Jewish context of seeing your job as what you do (to earn your portion, or *parnassa* in Hebrew), not as what you are, all that would be fun, but it wouldn't provide the soul food I get from being Mom, which is indeed what I am, not what I do.

And, while being Mom may not be as exciting as creating ice cream flavors, it isn't as dangerous either. I did get a shiver from that Ben and Jerry's story when the interviewer asked Mr. Douglas what flavors he had created, and he answered, "I actually have four flavors coming out, but unfortunately, if I told you what they were, I'd have to kill you."

Gee, you can have all my carpool secrets at no risk to your life at all.

By Erica Meyer Rauzin

The City Mouse and the Country Mouse

Two mice were cousins. One lived in the city and the other in the country. The city mouse decided to visit her country cousin. The country mouse was very excited to have a visitor from the city, so she prepared an elaborate meal. She set out the finest foods the country had to offer: fresh cheese, succulent roots, and crusty bread. The country mouse enjoyed the meal, but the city mouse ate sparingly, tasting just enough to be polite. Obviously, the city mouse was not impressed.

After dinner, the city mouse told many stories about her adventures in the city. When they went to bed, the country mouse dreamed of how exciting city life would be. The next morning, when her cousin asked her to come home with her and visit the city, the country mouse accepted eagerly.

When they arrived at the mansion the city mouse lived in, they quickly went into the dining room. The table was filled with a great feast: the finest imported cheeses, cream-filled pastries, dainty meats, and sweet desserts. The country mouse eagerly began eating everything. She started to feel that she'd been missing many good things by living a simple life in the country.

As the two mice feasted, they heard a meow at the door. They scurried quickly across the table and hid breathlessly. They crouched out of sight for a very long time, barely daring to breathe. Finally the cat left and they ventured back out. In minutes, they ran into the servants who came in to clear the table. They hid again, peeked out to eat at last, and were chased away in a panic by the family's dog.

They fled to the city mouse's den. The country mouse had barely caught her breath before she grabbed her suitcase. She looked at her cousin and said, "You may enjoy many luxuries I don't have, but I'm far better off living peacefully and quietly in the country. I would rather eat seeds and roots in peace than cream and pastries in terror."

By Aesop

134

Exuberance

Let enthusiasm radiate in your voice, your actions,
your facial expressions, your personality,
the words you use, and the thoughts you think.

Ralph Waldo Emerson

The Couch

Now imagine a Saturday afternoon, a little boy, and a very beat up piece of furniture.

The couch was probably beautiful when it was new. The upholstery was a pretty plaid in blocks of soft cream, tan, and white. We never saw the seat cushions, but we assume it had some, once upon a showroom. By the time the couch came to us, it was a mess.

This is not a furniture rehabilitation story, in which I cleaned, stripped, padded, and reupholstered. The couch remained a mess; in fact, it got worse. This is a story about the way little kids see happy possibilities most of us can't quite fathom.

Our town provides bulk trash pick up four times a year. A notice comes in the mail about a week before, and during that week piles grow on the swale in front of each house: packing boxes, tree trimmings, ancient files, old mattresses, and beat-up furniture. A certain recycling process exists. No one is too proud to claim a discarded roll of screening that might shelter some garden seedlings or a book someone else considers useless. I got an entire set of encyclopedias that way once. The science stuff was out of date, but the art history was just fine.

This time, our seven-year-old son claimed the couch.

The neighbors who live three or four houses down put the couch out by the curb. Cushionless as it was, it still called to our child. He loved the couch instantly. He didn't care that white batting poked out of one squared-off arm, or that some cat had shredded the upholstery on the legs. He ran home to tell us about it. In his eyes, it was beautiful. He wanted it in his room, and he wanted it NOW.

We grownups were not at all interested in an old couch. It could have termites. It could have fleas. Forget it, we said. "I'll put it in my room," he pleaded.

Never mind that his room already holds two beds, a desk, a dresser, several shelves full of toy cars, and—most of the time—a six-foot-high teepee; the whole idea was out of the question. Finally he began to understand. Teary-eyed, he asked, "Can I play with it in our yard?"

We had to relent. We told him we would pull it into our yard, and he could play with it for the weekend only. After that, it would go back on the bulk pick-up pile and that would be the end of it.

We were naive. We were dumb. We were out of touch with reality. We didn't have a clue.

Not only does our kid love this couch; every kid in the neighborhood loves this couch. Everything any mother in a five-block radius ever told a small child he or she could not do on the couch, the kids are doing on this couch. And, they are doing it barefoot and filthy. They stand on it, jump on it, turn it over, and hide under it. They eat there. They do homework there. They sit and visit, they cuddle with the dog, they doze, they bounce, they make up terrifying gymnastics routines starring the couch, usually rolling it over as they somersault. They cover it with blankets and make it a hideout. It is better, by far, than a swing-set. Amazing.

Of course, the couch does nothing for the looks of our front yard, which is plain at best, but not usually a dump. Seeing a couch in the middle of our lawn reminds me of the rural homes we used to drive by up in the Appalachians in the 1950s. Couches in the yard were not common, but you did see them now and then. I guess it was too hot to sit inside. But the couches never just sat there alone. Once a yard was invaded by furniture, it piled up. You'd find lawn chairs and wooden-spool tables and rocker-less rocking chairs. You might see a washing machine on the porch or a car on blocks. That's what our house looks like it needs now: a crank washer on the front steps and a faded '56 Chevy on concrete blocks. Make mine red and white.

Needless to say, the bulk pick-up truck has come and gone without the couch. Every time we mentioned letting them take it, a half-dozen kids started to wail. Instead, we are moving the couch to the back yard. We will be less humiliated, and they can play on it until it comes completely apart; I do not think that will take very long.

But the couch (and maybe the notion of the Chevy) brought another image to mind. A couple of nights ago, when I looked out the window at my son and his friends, drinking lemonade, sitting on the couch outdoors in the sunset, I was reminded of a story my parents told about a man they saw once in British Guinea. Today, the country is Guyana, but their visit was more than forty years ago.

Traveling between towns, the guide drove them past a shanty with a black Rolls Royce on blocks in the front yard. The car was magnificent, gleaming. The guide told them that the car was owned by a former chauffeur whose boss had died many years ago and left him the Rolls. The chauffeur could not afford to keep it running, but he cherished it. He polished it every afternoon when he got home from work. He brushed the upholstery and put fresh flowers in the holders by the windows. And at dusk, his friends would come sit on the soft velvet seats in the Rolls, drink beer, and visit with him. My parents figured he was the happiest man in the world.

Now, could you throw away the couch?

By Erica Meyer Rauzin

Fun

We have sought truth and sometimes perhaps found it.
But have we had any FUN?

Benjamin Jowett (1817–1893),
Greek scholar, master of Balliol College, Oxford

Where's the Beef?

David and his family dinner were all eating hamburgers when the phone rang. The caller was a telemarketer.

"Good evening," the caller said. "I'm calling to verify that your wife entered a drawing to win one hundred pounds of beef and to tell you about some of the specials we're currently offering."

A mischievous gleam flickered in David's eye. "Really?" he said. "I find that very interesting because we're vegetarians." He was chewing his hamburger as he spoke. "Do you ever feel run down or have low energy?"

The telemarketer answered, "Yes, as a matter of fact."

"Do you ever have digestion problems?" David asked.

"Why, yes!"

Then, David asked, "Have you ever considered becoming a vegetarian? Are you aware of its many health benefits?"

The beef telemarketer was so consumed with pondering her new life as a vegetarian and talking to David about it, that she ended the call without trying to sell him anything. She hung up saying, "Maybe I should become a vegetarian. Thanks!"

"Life's too short," David told me. "If you can't beat the telemarketing system you might as well have some fun with it."

As told to PJ

Earl & Hootie

An owl and a rooster sing....
Earl and Hootie have feathers—
But there the similarity ends.
They're not birds of a feather—
But they're still feathered friends.
Though...

[CHORUS]

Earl works early...Cock-a-doodle-do!
And Hootie works late...Hootie-hootie hoo!
Earl works early...Cock-a-doodle-do!
And Hootie works late...Hootie-hootie hoo!

Earl, he lives in a barnyard—
Hootie in a big oak tree
Earl, he works for a farmer—
Hootie, independently.

Earl gets up with the chickens,
Crowin' at the crack of dawn—
Earl, he sleeps like a log all day,
'Til the daylight's come and gone.

So those two had never met
'Til that fateful, foggy day
When they ran into each other
In a most dramatic way...

Earl fluttered from his rooftop,
Just as Hootie, he swooped down...
Ka-boom! Mid-air collision!
Feathers flyin', white and brown!

Well, they dusted off each other,
Made sure they were all right.
"How d'ya cock-a-doodle-do?"
"Pleased to meet you-hoo.
"Wasn't that a bumpy flight!"

Earl says, "Hootie, how 'bout some dinner?"
Hootie says, "Breakfast would be nice!"
Well, they both agreed on chicken feed
With a nice side order of mice!

So now you know my story—
It's time for my song to end—
About the Early Bird and the Night Owl,
Each other's feathered friend...
Though...
Earl works early...Cock-a-doodle-do!
And Hootie works late...Hootie-hootie hoo!

By David C. Perry

Giving

Happiness is a by-product of an effort to make someone else happy.

Gretta Brooker Palmer

Who Listens Anyway?

The phone rang at my desk. When I answered a woman on the other end of the line said, "Hi, this is Kelly. I just had to call and thank you."

Since I couldn't even remember Kelly, I certainly wondered why she was calling to thank me. Not that I didn't appreciate the gesture. She continued, "Today I enrolled in classes to get my teaching certificate. If I hadn't met you I wouldn't have done it."

All I could think was, "If only all my phone calls could be this pleasant."

Then I started trying to figure out where I'd met her and why she was enrolling in school because of me. Then I remembered Kelly had been a substitute teacher in one of the classes that had a Junior Achievement program. (I was working for Junior Achievement, a nonprofit organization that partners the business and education communities to teach kids about business and economics.)

Kelly spent several weeks substitute teaching for a teacher who was out on medical leave. When I met her she clearly loved teaching and the students actually learned from her. We were chatting one day and I asked, "Why don't you teach full-time?" She responded, "I have a degree in economics, but I don't have my teaching certificate." I immediately replied, "Why don't you get one? You obviously love teaching, are great at it, and the students are learning from you."

It was easy to see that Kelly would be one of those gifted teachers. The kind whose students would remember her even after they left school.

It'd been at least eight months since I'd spoken to her. I'd even forgotten the conversation. I mean, how often do we cheer someone

141

on to do something, but they never do it? Most people would rather think about their dreams than actually follow them.

Then it dawned on me, that more often than not, it's the words of wisdom or encouragement from people who briefly cross our paths, that often helps us the most when we are at one of life's crossroads. It's as if that's why our paths crossed in the first place.

It might be someone you're sitting next to on an airplane, someone you meet in an elevator, or the person who's in line at the grocery store. You never know where they'll turn up.

And some days you're blessed to be the messenger. You never know when your words are the catalyst that gives someone hope, inspiration, or the motivation to follow a dream. It's the *It's a Wonderful Life* theme in action.

On occasion you might even be more blessed, because you find out that something you said actually resonated for someone, and they call to share their excitement and enthusiasm with you.

PJ

The Calling

Joan of Arc had a calling; so did countless biblical sages and revered saints.

When we think of someone having a calling to a particular profession, cause, or action, we're likely to think of some mysterious mystical voice or vision that "speaks" to them.

But callings are rarely that mystical. You can have a calling to do just about anything: create, educate, explore, support, love, help, nurture, feed, entertain, build, lead, invent, discover, communicate, protest, preserve, fight for a cause, enlighten, travel, defend, research, celebrate, comfort, investigate, and on and on.

And you can fulfill your calling in any way you wish.

What's a calling feel like? A strong desire, that's often unexplainable. It can be triggered by even the most common events. The right stimulus can leave you feeling that pull with certainty and commitment: You have to do it; you won't be happy or fulfilled if you don't.

The next time you're in a Mom and Pop deli or coffee shop and you see the welcoming owners behind the counter, chances are they're living out a calling to be hospitable, to nurture, and give. The restaurant is merely the vehicle.

A computer programmer may have a calling to be a Little League coach, Big Brother or other volunteer who works with kids. Sometimes your calling and the way you earn a living are not related.

Marie felt a calling to become, of all things, a funeral director. She felt such a strong desire to help people that she was drawn to the profession because she could think of no other time when people were more vulnerable than when losing a loved one. They had no greater need for commiseration and comfort than when they were faced with arranging a funeral.

Mark's mother and father both worked in the arts, and he too was drawn to music, writing, theater, and film. A typical teenaged boy of the early 1970s, Mark wore his hair long, his bell bottoms frayed, and his smile wide, often from hiding on the roof of his family's apartment building indulging in the illegal, hand-rolled recreation made popular in that era.

Nobody was surprised when Mark, who was extremely talented, landed the lead role of Tevye in a high school production of *Fiddler on the Roof*. But everybody was very surprised when, after the last performance, Mark announced that playing Tevye had triggered a calling—not to Broadway, but to become a rabbi.

He's been one now for nearly two decades.

PJ

Grateful

Welcome everything that comes to you,
but do not long for anything else.

Andre Gide

Little Things, Big Things

When Laura answered the phone she was surprised that it was a collect call from her old friend Rebecca...from a hospital.

"Are you sitting down?" Rebecca asked her.

"Uh-oh," Laura said. "Are you okay?"

"I have a benign brain tumor," Rebecca announced matter-of-factly. "But it's on the surface and contained. They say surgery will take care of it."

"Oh, thank God that's all it is," Laura sighed and laughed.

Rebecca (brain tumor and all) laughed too, because she knew what kind of year Laura had just gone through.

Despite the fact that their whole group of acquaintances were only in their early forties, a number of Laura's closest friends had passed away recently, some from terminal diseases, some from sudden accidents. This call gave Laura a different perspective. She remembered to be grateful for not only the little things but even for what at first seemed to be a very unwelcome big thing.

She breathed deeply at this realization and blurted out, "I'm just so happy you're not calling to tell me that you're dead!"

As told to PJ

145

An Attitude of Gratitude

It was two days before Christmas and I was leaving town to visit my mother for the holiday, but stopped by Louise's home, my friend and mentor, to wish her a happy holiday and to drop off a gift. She was a retired widow who lived alone. This was the first year in all the years I'd known her that both her son's families would be coming home for Christmas. She was sooo thrilled.

Louise always loved to share the holidays with everyone, and she was a fastidious decorator. Lighting both inside and outside was her thing. She always left the twinkle lights up in the canopy of trees in her backyard, year around, because the pilots at the local Air Force base once told her they could look down on their approach and spot her lights as a landmark. It was quite a canopy of lights, almost a constellation.

I rang her bell and waited. No answer. I knocked and waited. Finally, I heard her coming to the door and ask, "Who is it?"

"It's me, Louise. Did I get you up?" It was almost 8 P.M., but she was seventy-six.

She let me in saying, "I've already taken off my wig and was just watching TV, relaxing after today." I'd brought her a breakfast ring, which she happily accepted, and asked me to put it in her kitchen then join her in her bedroom. She often told me I was the daughter she never had. I made myself at home regularly.

I joined her in her room saying, "I can't stay long; I'm on my way to Mother's for a few days. When are your sons coming in?"

"Tomorrow," she replied. Then she said, "I'm glad you came by. I went to the doctor today for this cough that I can't shake. As you know, I've had it since I had the flu last spring. And I even had to quit smoking to get over the flu. Well..." She paused and took a deep breath and looked deep into my eyes.

I knew what she was going to tell me.

"The doctor found a spot on my lungs with the chest x-ray." She pointed to her upper lobe, "Up here somewhere; about the size of a dime or smaller." He wanted her to have a biopsy the next day, but she declined due to her sons' arrival.

"I just want us to have a really happy holiday together again after all these years, without anything overshadowing it. What's wrong with that? That's OK isn't it?"

"Of course it's OK, Louise. Nobody would want to spoil this for you. But you do need to get a biopsy after Christmas. When do Dan and John leave? They may want to stay for your biopsy."

She didn't want to tell her sons until after they'd left, and she had her biopsy results. She wouldn't be talked out of it, either. She didn't want chemotherapy, but maybe surgery—maybe not, depending on the biopsy. She'd only gotten the results at 5:30 P.M. and had not spoken to anyone except the doctor.

I left my chair and crossed the room to hug her. She told me, "I'm so glad you're here. I've worked so hard getting everything ready for the boys visit and now this. I just don't think I can tell them and spoil..."

At that moment her doorbell rang.

"Oh! Who could that be?" she quipped, pulling away from me and wiping her eyes.

"I'll get it, Louise. I'll get rid of them and tell them you've gone to bed early and I'm just leaving. You just stay there." I answered the front door.

I shouted to Louise, "It's a huge UPS package!"

"Get a knife from the kitchen and bring them both here," she responded.

As she opened the two and a half foot cubed box, she took out a letter and began to read. Then she covered her mouth and began to chuckle. She looked at me, back at the letter, down at the box, back at me, and began to laugh out loud.

"What is it, Louise?" I asked, feeling out of the loop on this turn of events.

"It's..." and she couldn't finish because she was laughing so hard. She sputtered and snorted and hooted and cackled and finally managed to choke out these words:

"It's from Phillip-Morris...a thank you for all my hard work... assembling those 15,000 signatures for Smokers Rights this year [even though she'd quit smoking herself]...They sent me a box full of tobacco products! Can you believe it?"

And she laughed some more, until tears ran down her face. We both laughed at the irony of the day. Then in one of those precious moments she took a breath between chuckles and said, "God does have a sense of humor."

She hugged me before I left, wished me a happy holiday with my mother, and thanked me again for coming by. I told her I'd see her in a few days and I'd be happy to take her for her biopsy if she didn't want her sons to go, but I didn't want her to go alone. She said she'd think about it after they left. Then she thanked me again for being a part of her life and said, "It's been a really good life you know. I'm grateful for every minute of it. And I'm not afraid."

That hour passed quickly as I drove through the dark night to my mother's home to celebrate the season. I was thinking of how courageous Louise had been her whole life, the many obstacles she overcame. If anyone had a right to claim the throne of the "pity-pot" she did; but that wasn't her style, so she didn't go there.

Gratitude was her style. Dynamic action was her style. Graciousness was her style. And charity was her style. Louise told me that she regularly prayed, "Dear Lord, if I can't help them, please don't let me hurt them." She considered it an honor to serve others, and said, "No one gets to heaven without the helping hand of another." She was keenly aware of all those who helped her throughout her life. Keen was her favorite word. And she was grateful for every flower and brick in her yard, for the beauty it allowed her to share with others. She loved to share her gardens and lawns with everyone who stopped by her home. Receiving for the purpose of sharing was so very important to her; it afforded her opportunities for gratitude.

Louise was an inspiration to so many through her achievements and the way she lived her life. It wouldn't surprise me if she beat this stupid spot. I prayed for her.

Louise didn't tell her sons about the spot until after the biopsy. She asked me to accompany her for the biopsy; I was in the room when the doctor told her it was malignant. She declined chemotherapy, tried radiation, but eventually accepted chemo.

She lived almost seven months.

It was her attitude of gratitude, even at the little ironies, like receiving a box of tobacco products, even though she'd quit smoking, on the day she had just been told that she had a spot on her lung, that were the essence of her soul that many others hope to emulate.

By T. Dominy

Humor

The most wasted of all our days
are those in which we have not laughed.

Sebastein

Making a Difference

I used to work for a boss who was a tyrant. One day I made a big mistake on a project we were working on and he started yelling at me and said that I alone screwed up months and months of work in just four hours. I felt bad for a few seconds and then responded with, "See, I really can make a difference around here." Everyone cracked up, even our mean boss.

By Terrill Fischer

Fillings

At the dentist's office

[Sung to the tune of "Feelings"]

Fillings...Nothing more than fillings...
Doctor, I'll ignore your bad breath
If we could have a little chat.

Drilling...can be very jaw-bone chilling...
The Geneva Convention must have
Outlawed stuff like that!

Billing...You dentists make a killing...
But let's not get too literal—
I don't care about your fee!

Willing? It's not that I'm not willing...
Just give me a little something, Doc,
Before you stick those drills in me!

Freezing? Surely you must be teasing...
Seems to me that foot-long needle
Last time really hurt!

Feeling...my face lost all its feeling...
And I dribbled half my lunch
All over my new shirt!
But, gas me? You don't even have to ask me...
Just hook up the old "nitrous"—
It's always been a "hit"!

Giggling...I've finally stopped my wiggling...
Now you could amputate my tongue
And I wouldn't care a bit!

By David C. Perry

The Underground Clergy

A friend and I were talking about his recent trip to the dentist, when he casually made the comment, "My dentist is a rabbi." I laughed and replied, "Really. I guess that's a good combination. Your mouth is full so you can't talk anyway, you hear a sermon, and you don't have to go to services on Friday. Talk about killing two birds with one stone."

What a way to have a captive audience, I thought. My friend laughed and said, "Pam he's not really a rabbi."

Of course, that didn't stop my imagination. I'd read that the clergy is concerned because fewer people actually attend services, except those culturally specific holidays: Easter, Christmas, Yom Kippur, Eid, Diwali and the list goes on.

So I thought perhaps the clergy had decided to go where the people who needed their words of wisdom and compassion were. Your hairdresser was a nun, the man who carried out your groceries was a preacher, your local bartender was a priest, and your dentist was a rabbi.

The possibilities were endless. It's almost better than a sermon. You'd actually get personalized spiritual guidance for your problems.

Imagine, you've had a Murphy's Law day, and it's raining so you decide to catch a cab instead of walking. When you get in the cab driver asks, "So how was your day?"

You respond, "My boss has been a jerk, my wife doesn't think I can do anything right, and my mutual funds lost money. I think that about sums it up."

The cab driver just listens and offers a few words of wisdom here and there that make you feel better. Why is it that cabbies always make you feel better? It's only when you pay him that you realize he's part of the small branch of the underground clergy...Clergy Cab!

PJ

The Bald Knight

Once upon a time there was a knight who was growing old, and as often happens with old age, his hair fell out and he became bald. To cover this up, the knight wore a wig. One day when he was hunting with some friends, an unexpected gust of wind blew off his wig and exposed his shiny bald head.

His friends laughed. Even the knight himself laughed as loud as anybody, saying, "How did I expect to keep strange hair on my head when my own wouldn't stay there?"

From that moment on, the knight knew that although his hair was lost he still had his humor.

Aesop

Joyful

Joy is the feeling of grinning inside.

Dr. Melba Colgrove

The Greatest Show

No matter how "heavy" things get,
Elephants never forget
That ever since birth
On this marvelous earth
Life is the Greatest Show yet!

153

Love

There is only one happiness in life, to love and be loved.

George Sand (1804–1876), French writer

Long Voyage Home

This is a transcript of a live performance by David C. Perry at the 90th birthday party of his grandfather, Clifford Perry, on April 11, 1998. "Long Voyage Home," also known as "The Ballad of Clifford and Annabel," is based on a true story.

1927, Port of Liverpool.
Passengers gather at the dock.
"All ashore that's going ashore! All aboard!"
Trans-Atlantic steamer, the *Marloch*,
Trans-Atlantic steamer, the *Marloch*.

Nineteen-year-old Clifford, bound for Montreal
Younger brother Leonard in tow.
Heading home to Canada—two boys on their own.
Not a soul on board did they know,
There were ten days and an ocean to go.

Who knows who will befriend us,
Or where the waves will send us,
On our long voyage home.

They weren't the only people on the dock that day.

Eighteen-year-old Annabel from Nashville, Tennessee,
With her girlfriends and a chaperone.
Their ship had hit an iceberg on their way to Europe

So they needed the *Marloch* to take them home.
They stood giggling, contemplating the unknown.

Who knows who will marry us,
Or where the waves will carry us,
On our long voyage home.

Now of the two brothers, I guess you could say Leonard was the more
outgoing—gregarious—so it fell to him to kind of break the ice, as it
were. But before you knew it, the boys were talking to the girls and
the girls were talking to the boys and nature took its course. It
became apparent that Clifford and Annabel had a very special bond—
and the Marloch, over the course of a few hours and days, turned into
the original Love Boat. *It made the* Titanic *look like a life boat.*

Clifford and Annabel were falling in love.
Nothing had ever felt so right.
Holding hands and talking—staring at the wake
Churning out behind them in the night
Out into the darkness—out of sight.

Speaking of "out of sight," it was a little hard to get privacy on that
big boat, but there was this room where people would go to play
cards. Not strip poker, no. It was a more genteel age.

One night in the card room
The young couple hid.
She said, "Clifford, you may kiss me."
And he did!

Who knows who will befriend us,
Or where the waves will send us,
On our long voyage home.

Inevitably, the Marloch reached the shores of North America. They were met by their respective families. They said an emotional "good-bye," hoping it wasn't "good-bye" forever, and they vowed to keep in touch—not by e-mail, not by fax machine—the old-fashioned way, by writing letters. Remember letter writing? And they also decided to do something kind of unique and creative: They decided they would read verses from the Bible—a different verse from the Bible each night,— but they would each read the same verse as the other was reading it, those thousands of miles away, at the same time, as a special way to keep in touch across the miles. And letters...they wrote letters...every day for two years.

Inevitably they met other people; they got married to other people. They raised families and the families would get together every once in a while on vacation. They all got along famously. My dad remembers some of those trips. But, of course, there was always a very special place in each other's hearts for Clifford and Annabel. They had full lives, happy lives, successful lives. And then Pepe, Annabel's husband, died...

For 25 years, Annabel lived the widow's life.
Like seagulls over oceans, time had flown.
She never remarried—Then Clifford lost his wife—Nana—Edith.
And there they were, once again alone,
Children and grandchildren long since grown.

So they re-established contact, tentatively at first, not quite sure what everybody was going to think. They decided, "Why don't we take a cruise, for old times' sake?" And they thought, "I don't know,—what would the children think? Well, maybe if we were married ..." What an outrageous idea!

Sixty-five years after their shipboard romance,
In their eighties, but teenagers at their core,
Clifford and Annabel got their second chance:
They got married and their love had come ashore!

Who knows who will befriend us,
Or where the waves will send us,
On our long voyage home.
Who knows who will marry us,
Or where the waves will carry us,
On our long voyage home!

By David C. Perry

First Love

I had barely gotten in the door on a recent visit to a friend when she joyfully announced that she was in love with a guy named Christopher. She was grinning and her eyes were lit up like a Christmas tree. She was glowing.

"What do you like about him?" I asked.

She couldn't really answer. All she knew was that she liked the way she felt when she was around him, and that he had blond hair and blue eyes.

"Is he someone you might want to marry?" I asked.

"I'm not sure. All I know is that I'm in love with him."

"Does he know this?" I asked.

"No," she gleefully announced.

"If you haven't told him, who have you told?" I asked as she giggled.

"My girlfriends," she smiled.

Then she started to blush and I asked, "Why?"

"I'm embarrassed," she said.

"Why?"

"Because being in love can be embarrassing."

Then, with her big blue sparkling eyes she looked at me and said, "I don't think I'm ever going to get married. Can we go look at my fish now?"

Since London's barely five years old, we immediately went to look at the fish.

All she knew was that she was in love, it felt great, and she wanted to share her joy with everyone. I think there's a lesson in that for those of us who've had our hearts broken: Just allowing yourself to love without concern or worry about where it's going is the ultimate happiness.

PJ

Peaceful

Happiness is the harvest of a quiet eye.

Austin O'Malley

Coming to America, Again

Lynne stood on the bow of the enormous ocean liner that was taking her and her family back home to America after a summer trip to Europe.

As the ship made its way through New York harbor, little Lynne reached up to hold her seventy-year-old grandfather's hand.

"It was just the two of us standing on the bow," she recalls now, nearly thirty-five years later. "And then we saw it—the Statue of Liberty. I thought about how, so many years before, just barely into the 1900s, my grandfather saw that statue for the first time. He, too, was just a child. But the circumstances were very different. He was fleeing eastern Europe and immigrating to America."

As Lynne and her grandfather held hands and gazed at the Statue of Liberty, "Our eyes met and I knew he was thinking the same thing I was. This normally gruff man suddenly looked so at peace. It's my favorite memory of him."

As told to PJ

Become Yourself

In the heat of the battle
the eye of the storm
the answers to questions
are frequently born
when fear is a shadow
and doubt's a surprise
caught in the stillness
your wisdom gets wise

become yourself tonight
just be the one you are
unique in every way
you are a rising star
your life belongs to you
that is your destiny
become yourself tonight
the one you need to be

you are here
this is real
open up
learn to feel

this is life
understand
your happiness
is in your hands

just accept
what's happening
feel the moment
that you're in
this is real
you have arrived
feel the power
you have inside

you are strong
you are blessed
on the road
to happiness

feel the calm
the battle's won
on this day
that you become...

YOURSELF!

become yourself tonight
just be the one you are
unique in every way
you are a rising star
your life belongs to you
that is your destiny
become yourself tonight
the one you need to be

feel your own pulsation
and the life within your breath
listen to your heartbeat
live in every moment
and let every moment go
living in the moment
is the only way you'll know...

YOURSELF

become yourself tonight
and learn how life can be
as you feel your love
caress your dignity
your life belongs to you
to you and no one else
the heavens sing tonight
as you become yourself!

By Christine DeLorey

Playful

*You can discover more about a person in an hour of play
than a year of conversation.*

Plato

The Shoppers

My friend Kim had wanted a dog for a long time, so one
Saturday morning she went to a pet superstore that runs a
special pet adoption program. She played with several dogs and then
saw Brandi, a part Chow, part German shepherd. Brandi seemed a
little shy. But when Kim walked her around the store, Brandi led Kim
straight to the toy section. Brandi then proceeded to pull out all the
doggie stuffed animals she liked. It was one of the cutest things Kim
had ever seen.

"I knew immediately that Brandi was supposed to be my dog,"
Kim joked. "Because she's like me: Brandi is a shopper and she
knows exactly what she wants."

Kim and Brandi are living, playing, and shopping happily ever
after.

As told to PJ

Relief

*To overcome the difficulties is to experience
the full delight of existence.*

Arthur Schopenhauer

Entering the Twilight Zone

I was out of town at a business conference for a few days, and I
simply wanted to go to a mall to buy a few things I'd forgotten
to bring with me. It should've been an uneventful evening.

I finished my shopping just before the mall closed. Then, I headed
to the parking garage to find my rental car, a dark blue Oldsmobile
Achieva. About a mile into the drive back to my hotel, I looked at my
gas gauge and noticed it was almost empty. By my calculations, this
was impossible.

I had just filled the tank the night before. Today, I'd only driven
twenty miles from my hotel to the conference hotel where I had valet
parked. After the meetings, I'd driven a few miles to the mall. That
was it.

There was another discrepancy. When I had picked up the rental
car at the airport a few days earlier, it had only five-hundred miles on
it. When I saw that the gas tank was empty, I thought perhaps the
hotel's valet drivers had taken my car joy riding, so I checked my
odometer. It had 18,000 miles on it. Whoa! The valet only had it
seven hours. They hardly could have indulged in a 17,500 mile joy
ride!

I frantically looked around inside the car. You guessed it. It
wasn't mine.

Not quite thinking coherently, I searched for my rental car papers.
Of course, I found nothing; they were in my actual rental car. I began
to panic. I figured the valet must have given me the wrong car when I
left the conference hotel. I raced to my hotel. I figured I could call the
conference hotel, tell the valet to find my car, and ask him how I

could get this one back to its owner. I couldn't believe I was driving along in someone else's car and I didn't have a clue where my car was.

As soon as I pulled into my hotel's parking lot, I opened the back door to get my backpack, which I'd put in the back seat when I left the conference earlier. No backpack.

I was shocked and surprised. I felt like I'd slipped into the Twilight Zone. If the valet hadn't given me the wrong car, that meant that I took the wrong car from the mall. In a matter of moments, I'd become an unwitting auto thief. How could I have taken the wrong car? How could my rental car keys work in someone else's car? Had the owners discovered that their car was missing? Had they called the police? Was I about to be arrested? Had their keys worked in my rental car?

By this time, the mall had been closed for at least fifteen minutes. I immediately raced back there. All I could think was, How do I call my boss and ask, "Is bail money something I can expense?" I had visions of returning to the mall to find police officers swarming at the scene of the crime. Would the police believe my story? Would I be arrested? Where was my rental car? What if someone else had accidentally taken it? How would I find them?

The ten-minute trip to the mall seemed to take an eternity. When I arrived, the parking garage was almost empty. But no police were staked out, and I didn't see anyone frantically searching the area for their car. I reparked the Achieva in the same spot I had "stolen" it from.

My initial panic faded, only to be replaced by a new one: Where was my car? I ran all over the nearly empty garage looking for it, but no luck. As I searched, I passed two elderly women who were walking along. One pointed at the car I'd just parked and said, "I think we parked over this way." I returned their car just in time. I tried to say something, but for once in my life I was speechless. That was probably a good thing. The women kept walking toward their car without giving me a glance. But when I watched them head for the car, I noticed stairs.

I walked down one level, looked to the right, and with a sense of enormous relief, saw a dark blue car that looked like the one I'd just stolen. The same make, model, and color, it also had California license plates. I ran to it in great excitement and saw, to my additional relief, that my backpack was where I'd left it on the seat.

I had parked my rental car in the exact same spot as the car I'd just "stolen," but one level below. What were the odds of that? My heart pounded as I unlocked the door, got in, cranked it up, and gratefully left the garage.

My mind raced as I drove back to my hotel. Did those two women realize that I'd changed their radio station from classical to country western? Did they realize I'd moved the seat and mirrors? Were they having a "Twilight Zone" experience of their own, right now?

The shock didn't wear off for a couple of days, but when it did, I started thinking that the whole experience was pretty funny. Imagine finding the identical car, parked in the same space, but on another level. And the key fit. How often would I unknowingly steal a car, realize it, and return it without anyone knowing? Never again, I hope. To my relief, my brief career as a car thief has, thankfully, come to an end.

PJ

It Was a Dark and Stormy Night

Eleven P.M. Our dogs start barking loudly, with a note of warning. I look through the living room window blinds and see that the street in front of our house is flooded. I tiptoe into my sleeping daughter's bedroom, peer out of the window, and observe a man opening the fire hydrant.

He is tall and muscular, like someone who works out at a gym almost constantly. He is wearing jeans, a white T-shirt, and a baseball cap turned backwards. He is carrying a big wrench. After a few minutes, he uses the wrench to knock the hydrant knob closed, and walks up the street.

I don't know what you'd do (probably something more sensible), but I call the local police department. Don't misunderstand, I don't call 911; I know this is not an emergency, but I'm thinking that it is vandalism. I'm home alone with the kids and the sight of a big guy wandering about my neighborhood apparently breaking things with an even bigger wrench makes me uncomfortable.

I tell the switchboard person at the police department this little saga, and she says she'll send someone by to check it out. Sure enough, fifteen minutes later (well, it's not an emergency), a policeman pulls up on a motorcycle. The guy with the wrench is long gone, but the street is still flooded, though the water is receding fast.

I go out to talk to the cop. I thank him for coming. He looks at me like no one ever did that before, gestures to my neighbor's car curbside, and announces, "I'm going to have to ticket this car, and if you don't move it, I'm going to tow it."

I am, you might say, somewhat taken aback.

"It's not my car; it's my neighbor's car," I say, "and I called you because I thought someone was vandalizing the hydrant."

That hydrant. The one my neighbor's car is parked in front of, the one that flooded the street.

"The fire department comes around once a year and flushes the hydrants, so things don't back up or get rusty," the officer says. "The guy called us and said someone from your house had noticed him and might have been alarmed. He told us what he was doing."

Pity he didn't tell me.

So now my dangerous marauding vandal is a firefighter—without a uniform, without a city truck (parked, it turned out, so far up the street where I couldn't see it). And, my heroic source of rescue and comfort is about to tow my neighbor's car.

"But, but, but," I sputter, "You can't tow their car. I called you."

"I'm going to ticket it, because it's blocking the hydrant, and then I'm going to knock on their door, and if they aren't awake or won't move it, I'm going to have to tow it," he says.

I go back inside to phone my neighbors. I figure they'd rather be woken up than towed. Then my husband pulls up in his car, home late from midnight duty at the office. By the time I fill him in, the policeman has rung the neighbor's doorbell, and everybody is up.

The cop leaves the ticket on their windshield and departs without further conversation, apparently unwilling to discuss the morality of ticketing conducted by an invited guest.

Now if the firefighter had been wearing a uniform, or if the switchboard operator at the police station had said, "That's just the fire department flushing the hydrants," or if the dogs hadn't barked, none of this would have happened. No harm done, you say. Sure, but I've offered to split that $28 ticket.

By Erica Meyer Rauzin

Satisfaction

*Happiness does not come from doing easy work
but from the afterglow of satisfaction
that comes after the achievement
of a difficult task that demanded our best.*

Theodore I. Rubin

A Few Good Tears

It was Hannah's last semester of college and she was still wondering, "What do I want to do when I grow up?" For now, practicing law was leading the pack, so she was researching law schools and preparing to take the LSAT.

When she went home one weekend to visit her parents in Raleigh, North Carolina, she and her dad went to an air show. She'd always loved planes and was fascinated by the military. Her dad and grandfather were both veterans of the armed services. They had always shared stories about how much they learned in the military, the advantages that Americans had compared to people in other countries, their love for the United States, and the pride they felt because they'd had the opportunity to serve their country. So, growing up, Hannah developed a great sense of patriotism.

The air show was full of military personnel. Hannah hadn't really considered a career in the military because she had never known a woman who'd served. That day her perception changed. She found out that she was eligible to enter officer training. The thought of serving the country she loved so much overwhelmed her; she knew she had to pursue it.

She broached the subject of joining the Air Force or Navy with her parents. They were supportive and proud of her. They believed it would be a good career move and a learning experience. The only advice her mom jokingly gave her was, "Just don't join the Marines." "Don't worry, I won't," said Hannah.

She went back to school in Johnson City, Tennessee, to finish out the semester and started talking to military recruiters from the Air Force, Navy, and Army. A college friend in the Marine Reserves suggested that she should consider talking to a Marine recruiter. Hannah laughed and said, "Are you nuts? The Marines aren't my style."

Her friend said, "No, they're exactly your style."

With a little nudging, he set up a phone appointment for her with a recruiter. The phone recruiter called her and asked if she could set up a meeting with the Marine officer who interviewed potential officer candidates. Hannah still wasn't convinced she should even bother to interview because she'd never pictured herself as a Marine. She was still a typical southern girl, who liked to curl her hair, polish her nails, and match her belt and shoes. The Marines didn't even vaguely match this image. When the recruiter asked Hannah whom she'd spoken with she replied, "The Army, Navy, and Air Force."

He said, "Just meet with us. That way you'll always know you've exhausted every avenue before you make your choice." That comment closed the sale, and she agreed to meet with Captain Simmons, that July, when he was in Johnson City.

A few weeks later, Hannah met with the captain. Initially she thought he was very cocky. To her surprise, however, within five minutes of the meeting, she was ready to sign on the dotted line and begin her career as a Marine. In that brief time, Captain Simmons had demonstrated a love and enthusiasm for serving his country that Hannah hadn't experienced when she'd met with the other recruiters. She almost instantly knew with her heart and soul that the Marines were the place for her.

She immediately began the lengthy, tedious application process. The officer training program had only two open spots for female, college graduates from Tennessee. The selection process would be competitive, but den it was the Marines.

Hannah would have to take a series of tests and pass them before her application would be sent to the commandant's office in Washington, D.C. In August, after she graduated, she took the physical, running a mile and a half in ten to thirteen minutes, doing fifty sit-ups in under a minute, and performing a flex arm hang. She failed. She began an intense physical training program. In September, she took the physical test again and passed, but she wanted to pass with a higher score, so she waited and continued training. Finally in February, she'd passed all of the tests with high marks and submitted her application.

After graduation, she'd taken a crummy job working as a skip tracer, because she didn't want to begin working in a more professional career, only to quit in a few months to go to boot camp.

In March, she finally received notice that her application had been forwarded to Washington, D.C. She'd know within a couple of weeks if she would be admitted to the Marine Corps Officer Training Program.

She celebrated her 23rd birthday in April with her family at her grandparents' home. She was scheduled to meet with the Marine recruiter later that evening. The mail arrived and Hannah's mother brought her a letter from the Marines. Since she'd been in transition, she'd listed her grandparents' house as her permanent mailing address. Hannah knew it was her moment of truth. Everything she'd spent the last year working for was either about to happen or she was in for the biggest disappointment of her life. Her hands were shaking; she held her breath as she opened the letter and began to read.

Tears ran down her cheeks as she read aloud to her family, "You've been accepted into the Marine Corps Officer Training Program." Her dreams were about to become reality.

As she was leaving to meet with Captain Simmons, her grandfather walked her to her car. He handed her the compass he used in World War II. "If you're going to be a Marine, you'll need this," he told her.

Her grandfather's gesture of love and pride again prompted a few good tears as she drove off, completely overwhelmed: the few, the proud—the happy, teary, soon-to-be—Marine.

As told to PJ

Just Call Me Santa

Although Lorraine considers herself to be a very happy person, she has few close friends. In the past she would receive a few gifts during times of celebration, such as birthdays and Christmases but always wanted more.

So this year, Lorraine decided to set aside everything she mail ordered from October to Christmas. She would keep the boxes sealed when they arrived, gift wrap them or have them gift wrapped by the mail order companies, and place them under the Christmas tree.

"I would label each one, To: Lorraine, From: Lands' End, or whatever company I received the gift from," Lorraine said. "I only did this with mail order because I haven't really seen it, so it'd be somewhat of a surprise when I open the boxes."

"By Christmas Eve, the rug under my tree was piled with packages," Lorraine said. "This was my best Christmas ever! Not only did I get many more gifts, I also got exactly what I really wanted! I'm going to do it again for my birthday."

It's not true that you "can't get no satisfaction." You can. Sometimes you just have to get it for yourself.

As told to PJ

Spiritual

To live happily is an inward power of the soul.

Marcus Aurelius

A Moment in the Middle of Nowhere

My southwestern business trip included a weekend stay, so I decided to see the sights. I was particularly interested in hiking in the desert to some ancient Indian ruins. At a cafe, I talked to a local man who drew a map on a napkin showing me how to reach the "oldest most sacred ruins." He warned, "Most folks don't go see these ruins, because they're off the beaten path. It's several miles from the paved road and some of the turns are based on landmarks. There aren't any street signs in these parts."

Always up for an adventure, I headed there the next morning. Once I got off the pavement and starting driving on the dirt roads, I kept seeing signs that said "steep hills." I decided I should park my rental car, which wasn't exactly designed for steep dirt roads. I realized that if I happened to get stuck in a sandy ditch, I couldn't count on getting a tow truck to pull me out.

By my calculations based on the "map," I was only about a mile from the site. I certainly could hike that far. I parked and started walking. After about an hour, which meant I'd walked more than a mile from my car, I found the ruins and hiked around them for a while.

The ruins offered an interesting glimpse of history, typical of their period: cave dwellings with critters, dirt floors, and sketches that resembled chalk figure drawings, except they were a few hundred years old.

Since I hadn't planned on such a long hike I didn't have any supplies with me. No water or food, not even a hat. Before too long, I was ready to find air conditioning, water, and a shower. The sun was burning brightly, and it was getting hotter by the minute. The area was very desolate. I only saw one other car after I parked mine, and there were only a couple of other people exploring the ruins.

I started walking the long dirt road back to my car. It was hot. I was getting tired and thirsty. I could hear wildlife on both sides of the road. Sometimes my heart skipped a beat if I let my imagination get out of hand at the sound of some rustling in the brush. What if there was a snake? What if it bit me? What would I do?

I kept walking. With every hill I climbed, I anticipated seeing my car just over the rise, but I never did. I started to get frustrated, and hotter, and thirstier. The trip back to the car seemed to be taking much longer than the walk to the ruins. I searched for landmarks that would tell me I was approaching my car. I was too busy looking in the distance to pay attention to where I was putting my feet, so I tripped.

I fell hard, but fortunately, only skinned my knee. That was enough to jolt me back to reality. Clearly, I needed to pay attention to the steps right in front of me instead of gazing over the horizon. If I didn't, I could take a real fall, sprain an ankle, trip over a snake or some other critter, and get stuck on this dirt road waiting for help that might never come.

If I just kept walking, and was a little more careful, I'd eventually end up at my car.

Then it dawned on me that life works this way too. When we know what the goal is that we're heading toward, sometimes we spend so much time looking toward it in the distance that we forget to pay attention to the necessary steps in front of us. That's when we trip, fall, and get delayed or wander off our path.

And then I saw my car, right where I had left it. In moments, I was in motion, in air conditioning, and on my way to a cold iced tea, a late lunch, a hot shower, and a long nap.

I'd had an enlightening day. I got to see how people lived in dirt caves, which certainly makes one appreciate modern housing. My real lesson, though, was a reminder to watch the steps in front of me, because that's how I would finally reach my destination.

PJ

Surprise

Each day comes bearing gifts. Untie the ribbons.

Ann Schabacker

The Southern Belle at the Fish Fry

Back in high school, I was in the 4-H club. I was looking
forward to receiving an award at the county's annual banquet
that year. As they did every year, the Kiwanis Club sponsored the
banquet. They held a fish fry to pay for the banquet and to fund some
other projects, and asked the 4-H award winners to volunteer to be
their free labor at the fish fry. My parents, who were trying to instill
good values in me, thought I should volunteer.

Since I was a bit of a southern belle, the thought of working at a
fish fry wasn't my idea of fun, or anywhere near it. In fact, I asked if
the fish fryers were violating child labor laws. My parents informed
me that I was going to volunteer, and therefore it wasn't child labor.
Sulky, I knew there had to be some kind of name for involuntary
volunteering since I was being forced to do this by parental fiat.

On Saturday morning, Forced Fish-Fry Volunteer Day arrived. I
figured I'd be taking tickets or refilling iced tea. I began to think,
"Okay, so how bad could it be?" Maybe I'd even meet a cute guy who
was also being forced into fish fry labor. My mom dropped me off at
8 A.M. to begin my four-hour shift. I was given my assignment. To
my shock and disgust, I was part of the fish-battering team. I couldn't
believe my mother would leave me there to batter raw, stinky fish. All
I could think was, "Could I get a disease from this? And it's so gross,
what about my nails?!"

Before Mom left, I not so politely informed her that she'd better
not be a minute late picking me up. I wanted out of there exactly at
noon. I'm sure I had an afternoon of extremely important shopping to
do, or extremely important phone calls to make to my girlfriends.

I began my sentence. I put on the plastic gloves and the hair net and started battering smelly catfish with cornmeal and putting it in baskets to be fried. I'm certain my disgusted attitude was more than obvious. I began to wonder if my parents called and suggested that I be given this particular job. They were determined to keep me from becoming a complete prima donna.

To my surprise, however, soon enough I was talking, laughing, and tossing fish and batter around with the other fish fryers. I was actually enjoying myself. Before I knew it, it was noon. As promised, my mother was there exactly on time to pick me up. There was only one problem: I was so happy and having so much fun that I begged her to leave and pick me up later. She said, "No." She also wouldn't let me take a cab, so, to my disappointment, I went home with her.

Those afternoon pursuits that seemed so important to me earlier had lost all their urgency and appeal. I wanted to play at the fish fry. I realized that day that you never know when or where you'll find happiness. If you just get out of your own way, happiness can surprise you anywhere, even in a vat of fish batter.

PJ

Sweet

What sunshine is to flowers,
smiles are to humanity.
They are but trifles, to be sure,
but scattered along life's pathway,
the good they do is inconceivable.

Joseph Addison

Something's Funny in First Grade

My son has developed a sense of humor intelligible only to another six-year-old, and to his teacher.

"Do you know why I love my teacher?" he asked me.

"Why?" I responded.

"Because when you tell him, 'Say something funny,' he says, 'Something funny,'" my child giggled with delight, cracking up at his high level of wit and wisdom.

I don't call it wisdom lightly. It takes a certain amount of insight on the part of a six-foot-plus-tall adult to understand humor from the perspective of someone less than one-third his height, not to mention age.

I was reminded of the old New York joke where one guy says, "Call me a cab." And the other guy says, "Okay, you're a cab." And they both double-step off stage to the musical cadence of "Jadda Jadda Jing Jing Jing."

But this isn't vaudeville, this is first grade, where this teacher's kind sense of humor enables him to impart a great deal of solid information to a very young audience.

The teacher spends much of his day sitting on little bitty kiddy chairs, bending down to listen to small children at the height of their eyes and ears, and stooping to retrieve and replace the things they keep dropping, including backpacks, lunch boxes, and baseball caps. Of course, he is prepared for this. He has a master's in special ed, tremendous talent on the piano and on the computer, and a young back. It's a good thing he's young, or he'd have to retain a chiropractor to follow him around all day keeping his spine intact. How he remains so good humored in the face of permanent pretzeling is beyond me.

I also give him tremendous credit for his understanding of his core audience.

Sometimes, my understanding isn't as keen.

About two weeks ago, my son was fretful about a little stage play that his class might be doing. The very idea of performing in public made him nervous, so I tried to tell him that he should stay calm until he knew whether the show would even occur. I advised him that anticipating problems was making him unhappy, perhaps unnecessarily. The phrase I used was, "Don't borrow trouble."

Never use a cliché with a little kid, because it leads you to other clichés. As this discussion continued, I inadvertently led myself into, "Don't count your chickens before they hatch." I thought it provided just another way of showing my son that he ought to wait until he knew what was going to happen before he got upset. I explained this concept in detail. He seemed to accept setting his worries aside until he knew more about what was actually going to happen.

He even seemed content with my explanation, until my husband got home. When Daddy asked our son how his day had been, I found out what the child really thought. "It was good," he said. " I was worried about a show we might do at school, but Mommy told me, 'Don't borrow chickens.'

"Do you know why else I love my teacher?" my child asked again, later.

"Why?" I responded, in my new guise as Mom, the second banana.

"Because when you tell him, 'I'm thirsty,' he says, 'Hi, thirsty. Good to meet you.'"

Jadda, Jadda, Jadda Jing Jing Jing

By Erica Meyer Rauzin

About the Writers

The stories in this section bylined "PJ" are mine. The other writers whose work appears here are highly regarded journalists, essayists, and humorists, each with a unique take on the varieties of happiness. Permissions and publications acknowledgments for their included works appear at the end of the book.

Aesop is, well, you know who Aesop is!

Christine DeLorey is a world-renown numerologist (www.numerology.freesoul.com) and author of *Life Cycles: Your Emotional Journey to Freedom and Happiness* (Osmos Books).

T. Dominy is a singer/songwriter, grandmother of three, living at Lake Tahoe working on her Gram T Series of children's books. Her diverse background is surpassed only by her zest for life.

Terrill Fischer is the Dean of Humor for Humor University (www.humoruniversity.com). He describes himself as a "recovering serious person." He's a professional standup comedian performing at comedy clubs and corporate events all over the country.

David C. Perry, a talented art director and musician based in Philadelphia, performs his song parodies for lucky friends and the occasional coffee house audience.

Erica Meyer Rauzin is an editor and writer with an extensive journalism background. Her humor column runs in Jewish community newspapers nationwide. Her writings presented here will appear in her upcoming book, a compilation of her columns, which will never actually exist if she doesn't clean up her office and get started.

Tell Us Your Happy Story

If you'd like to submit a happy story to be considered
for publication on our web site (www.sohp.com)
or in our newsletter *Carpe Diem* send it to:

Secret Society of Happy People
5330 N. MacArthur Blvd.   Suite 148-215
Irving, Texas   75038

or e-mail: happystories@sohp.com

or fax: 972-745-7163

Be sure to include your full name, mailing address,
day time phone number and e-mail address.

Epilogue

Most people are about as happy as they make up their minds to be.

Abraham Lincoln

Ironically, as I finish this book I recognize that much of the focus in Part One is on the absurd, annoying, and sometimes unpleasant but always funny adventures of the Society. It may even have minimized the fact that a large number of journalists and other people understood, appreciated, and supported the message of the Society. There are lots of people who are members of the Secret Society of Happy People, either in spirit or the actual card-carrying kind.

People embrace the Society's message because it represents something they already know. It's better to share happiness than keep it a secret.

It's exciting to see that the newest daytime talk shows have variety show formats: fun and entertainment. Even our recent infatuation with evening game shows represents our interest in play and even borrowed happiness (we really are happy when they win all that money, even if for a moment we wish it had been us).

It's impossible to capture the feeling you have when an idea that came to you out of the blue starts to crystallize and people embrace the message. Every day, I get to interact with people who are enthusiastic and feel we need to express more of our happy moments. That, of course, begins by recognizing them.

It takes a brave person to live a happy life. That's because happiness isn't the absence of pain, annoyance, or the mundane. But happiness is a soulful experience. That's why everyone tries so hard to find it. However, once you recognize happy moments; our culture doesn't support you just enjoying them. This past year made me even more aware of this reality and more committed than ever that our culture needs the Secret Society of Happy People.

Every day is a new adventure. But every adventure, including the semi-annoying ones, is an opportunity to encourage people to talk more about happiness and discourage parade-raining. It's reminding people that even roses have thorns and pretty petals and it's up to each person to decide which of these they want to focus on.

The Society's journey has just begun, and with any new journey into uncharted waters it's rarely smooth sailing all the way.

The Society will continue to advocate for the expression of happiness in a public forum because for every person who becomes a member, or wants to wear our "stuff," there are perhaps millions who've just read about us in a newspaper or magazine, or on the internet, or heard about us on the radio, or saw us on TV, or a friend told them about us. And you never know which of these people will recognize a happy moment, share it, or embrace the happy news of someone else with enthusiasm or at the very least forgo raining on someone else's parade. And then there are the people who already live that philosophy and are just happy to know that others believe in it too.

It's for all of these reasons that the Society will continue working toward making the language of happiness chic, once again.

All beings are seeking happiness. It is the purpose of life.

The Dalai Lama

About Us

The Secret Society of Happy People was formed in August 1998 to encourage the expression of happiness and discourage parade-raining. Parade-rainers are those people who don't want to hear your happy news.

Somewhere between the *Ed Sullivan Show* and the *Jerry Springer Show* talking about being happy became politically incorrect. We're more comfortable airing our dirty laundry than telling people we've had a happy moment and listening to "woundology" than happy news.

"Woundology" became the intimacy language of the 1990s according to Caroline Myss, author of *Anatomy of the Spirit*. We spend most of our time repeatedly discussing things like "My boyfriend is a jerk," "If I'd only had more money," and "I need to buy something." We imply, and think, if these things happen or change we'd be happy.

The Society believes you have a right to be happy and talk about it without people rolling back their eyes, ignoring you, and even telling you in a snide tone, "That only happens to you" or "I don't want to hear it."

We believe happiness is contagious and that when more people talk about happy events and moments, it will be chic for everyone to do it.

The Society gained international recognition in December 1998 when it challenged Ann Landers for discouraging people from writing happy holiday newsletters to enclose with their holiday cards. Since then the Society has announced the Top Ten Happy Events and Moments of 1998 and 1999, honored Three Prominent Crusaders "For Not Letting Anyone Rain on Their Parade," and is supporting the ACLU in an effort to educate and lobby for laws protecting free speech in the workplace (including the expression of happiness), declared August 8 as National Admit You're Happy Day, and organized voting for the Happiest Events, Inventions and Social Changes of the Century.

The Society was featured in *People* magazine (August 30, 1999), founder Pam Johnson was on *Politically Incorrect with Bill Maher*

(March 1999), and *Glamour* magazine (May 1999) mentioned the Society in an article. Hundreds of print and broadcast outlets throughout the world have covered the Society, including CNN, the Associated Press, *Fort Worth Star-Telegram*, the *Dallas Morning News*, the *Los Angeles Times*, and the *Washington Post*. *Parade* named our Happiest Events, Inventions, and Social Changes of the Century as the Best List of the Century (December 26, 1999).

The Secret Society of Happy People's web site includes happy stories and other happy boosters (www.sohp.com). The Society also offers a unique line of merchandise: sweatshirts, T-shirts, coffee mugs, umbrellas and other happy stuff including charter memberships into the Society.

Professional resources available include:

When You're Happy and You Know It...Tell Someone: Identifying the Types of Happiness

A curriculum designed to help participants in living skill and wellness programs identify and express happiness.

Don't Even Think of Raining on My Parade

A program for companies and organizations to implement that encourages the expression of happiness in the workplace.

Founder Pam Johnson is also available for presentations.

If you'd like more information you can contact the Society through:

Web site: http://www.sohp.com
Phone: 972-471-1485 or 800-291-3068
Fax: 972-745-7163
Mail: 5330 N. MacArthur Boulevard, Suite 148-215
Irving, Texas 75038

Partial proceeds of sales benefit the Secret Society of Happy Kids, a nonprofit organization.

About the Author

Pam Johnson is the founder of the Secret Society of Happy People, the consumer advocate for the right to express happiness. The Society encourages the acceptance of expressing happiness and discourages parade-raining.

She also founded the Secret Society of Happy Kids, a non-profit organization that develops programs, for schools, youth groups and parents to facilitate happy expressions.

Pam is a writer, motivational speaker, and workshop facilitator.

As president of PJ Communications, she assists companies in developing and implementing marketing, sales, and public relations plans. She has also worked as a regional marketing representative for a major publisher, in event planning, public relations, and coordinating training programs for corporate and education professionals, and in fundraising.

She lives in Coppell, Texas, a Dallas suburb, where she is often happy, proud to admit it, and tries not to rain on anybody's parade.

Permissions